THE ORIGINAL MILLENNIAL

Lessons in Leadership for the Millennial Generation

Kini,

Always an original!

THX

Aerial Ellis

© 2015

Aerial

ISBN: 1516922646
ISBN 13: 9781516922642

Preface

1992. The evening news was on TV. I heard the anchor say something about scientists and researchers predicting that the world may end by the year 2000 – the next millennium. I had never heard that word "millennium" before. I knew I would be graduating from high school in the year 2000. I kept envisioning how the arena would explode into flames during my graduation ceremony (if the world was truly going to end at that time). No traditional pomp and circumstance. No cap and gown donning. No tassel turned to the right. No grip-and-grin photo with my high school principal. I kept thinking what life would be like after 2000 because certainly no one really knew when the world would come to a complete and absolute end, right? I thought maybe life would be like The Jetsons cartoon. I just couldn't imagine writing the date without '19' in front of the year. I wondered what the future held. I didn't know what would come of my generation. I thought people of my generation had to be something special if we would be the generation to become adults at the turn of a new century. But I was just 9 years old. I was confused. I was hopeful. I was aware. I was a millennial.

Fast forward to 1997. I had become fascinated with anything girly. I had also become interested in how businesses work. I would accompany my mom to the hair and nail salons as she visited for her regular appointments each month. The women who owned the salons were also the service providers in charge of beautifying their patrons. This amazed me. Not only did they have the skills to doll up anyone who stepped foot in their shop, they also had the business savvy to run a successful and thriving operation. I would watch them work then go home and mimic their style. I soon taught myself to give manicures and pedicures that were professional salon quality. I set up shop in my kitchen and would take clients on the weekends, after school and during the summer. Some months I would make nearly $500 giving manicures and pedicures to friends, family, church members and even people I didn't know who were referred to me. Although I was too young to be licensed I had officially launched my first entrepreneurial venture. I was 14.

Each week my mom would take me to Golden Beauty Supply to stock up on supplies. The store, like many of the beauty supply stores popping up around that time in predominately black neighborhoods, had every possible ethnic beauty and hair care product any woman of color could want. Aside from the variety of products, there was one thing that remained the same at each beauty supply store. They were all owned and operated by Koreans.

I couldn't understand why the owners of stores who sold products for mainly black women who looked like me didn't have hair texture or skin tone like mine. How well could they sell a product they never used? How well could they possibly know their customers or the issues in communities where their stores were located? At that age I understood that all people no matter their ethnicity should have the right and access to own their businesses in any community they choose and to generate wealth for their families. But I couldn't help ask why? Why is this so, why is this the norm and why don't these businesses help to improve the wellbeing of the communities where they conduct business? I was curious. I was engaged. I was enterprising. I was on to something. I was 14 years old going on 15. I was a millennial.

IT ALL STARTED WITH A CULTURAL SHIFT

In the mid 1960s, black women typically bought their hair care products from Walgreens, Woolworth or the neighborhood drugstore. But when black homeowners began to integrate with predominantly white neighborhoods, white families fled in mass, which sparked a cultural shift sociologists call "white flight." Oddly enough, during that same time, the Korean government banned the export of raw hair, making it impossible for U.S. business owners to manufacture wigs. Not long afterward, the U.S. government banned the import of any wig that contained hair from China. As a result, Korean business owners were able to dominate supply and distribution of weaves, wigs, extensions and ethnic hair care products. The shops abandoned by whites left an opportunity for immigrant entrepreneurs, such as Koreans, to start businesses like beauty supply stores that catered to the neighborhoods' new black population.

Let's go back to 1997. In 1997, African Americans had a total purchasing power of $469.4 billion. Today, African Americans spend approximately $500 billion on beauty and hair care. Forty-six percent of black households shop at beauty supply stores and spend on average $94 on products and supplies. And while this cultural shift shows the tremendous spending power of African Americans, hardly any of that cash makes it back to the black community.

Let's look deeper. Money circulates an unlimited amount of times among Caucasians, 9 times among Asians and 6 times among Latinos. Money circulates zero to one time within the Black community. Let's go even further. A dollar circulates in Asian communities for a month, Jewish communities approximately 20 days, Caucasian communities 17 days. A dollar circulates only six hours in the black community, according to Nielsen.

These statistics, as well as data related to crime, police brutality, race relations, education housing or employment, are the kinds of cultural changes that should always make us ask why?

Imagine a world in which everyone's ideas are valued and business risks are made to support high-potential, dynamic leaders as they realize their dreams and solve problems within their communities. Shifting the norm has been integral to cultural movements. It's how change occurs. Culture is a way of life. Culture is organic. Culture emerges. But it can also shift. It can change. It can make us thoughtful, purposeful and responsible around the behaviors, values, attitudes, beliefs and assumptions that we have in common.

For instance, if we look at the ways the civil rights movement of the 1960s functioned—the era that ushered a shift that made U.S. neighborhoods multicultural—it's undeniable that culture was at the center of those world-changing efforts. The results of the movement brought about change in the racial and ethnic makeup of our communities, the schools we attended and the businesses we had access to. And now, the globalization of education, politics, music, technology and even the latest civil rights movement of #BlackLivesMatter that emerged from social media have changed the way we live and as a result our patterns of competence, communication and consumption have shifted dramatically.

Much like those elements of culture, we are experiencing a shift within generational phases. We are seeing a shift among baby boomers (born 1946-1964) and members of Generation X (born 1965-1979) as the leading voices in business and the greater community. The so-called legends and power brokers from those generations aren't the only ones responsible for creating the most exciting things impacting our culture these days. Increasingly, millennials (born 1980-1995) are having the biggest impact on business culture.

This special breed of individuals, debunking myths and assumptions, will lead a cultural shift to represent fully 75 percent of the U.S. workforce by the year 2025, thus changing the face of business leadership. It's not surprising that the originality of millennials has created an era of leaders and entrepreneurs who measure success in social value rather than profits.

They see citizens as sources for solutions rather than as problems. They are risk-takers sharing a common thread of ensuring continuous improvement by discovering new ways of thinking and acting. And the hub of this entrepreneurial spirit lives within the heart of millennials.

But why is that change so hard for some to believe? Why is change, specifically generational change, so difficult to accept? Because change is complex. There's frustration from tensions between older and younger generations. There's resistance derived from hostile interactions and environments. There's anxiety from underutilization or lack of resources. There's confusion from misinformed stereotypes and perceptions.

Therein lies a relationship between cultural change and social entrepreneurship. Cultural change exposes problems by disrupting a system. This is a result of generations asking why. Social entrepreneurship solves problems by disrupting a system. This is a result of generations asking, why not? Millennials are doing more than running their businesses and giving back here and there. Instead, they make changing the hearts and minds of a community part of their business model. Millennials are doing more than clocking into a humdrum job and then clocking out to crash on their couches and watch TV for the rest of the night. Instead, they are burning the midnight oil working on their own ventures and contributing time to causes that impact the masses.

They are the millennials who are more ambitious to fuel cultural change than gain personal wealth and advancement. They have a distinctly original quality that debunks the labels of "slacker" or "narcissist" that are constantly slapped on millennials.

They are creative, innovative, enterprising, influential, bold, unapologetic and ready to solve the world's problems. They are called the original millennials.

The millennial generation is bigger and more diverse than any other generation. Most original millennials who were born in the early 1980s went through college only to find ourselves dissatisfied with our jobs, hopping from gig to another more frequently than our parents, grandparents and even older siblings. We took jobs in fields unrelated to our area of study. We became more likely to start our own businesses or entrepreneurial ventures and less likely to stay in an unfulfilling work environment than previous generations. We became invigorated by the ways that business can go well and do good at the same time. If we were unsatisfied with our jobs or communities, we became relentless in finding a better situation even if we had to create it ourselves.

Contrary to what is said or perceived, the original millennial is not lazy and selfish lacking motivation and creativity. The original millennial is a servant, innovator, go-getter—a leader. As the fastest growing generation, we've become leaders of the social entrepreneurship sector that emerged around 2007, when most of us graduated college or started our careers. Many millennials have been inspired by a cultural change to create organizations and movements that are neither businesses nor charities, but rather hybrid entities that generate revenue in pursuit of social goals.

Now there are tens of thousands of social ventures and many are being led by original millennials. To be sure, there are segments of original millennials shifting the organizational culture within the corporations they serve. The original millennial believes that solutions of the past won't work to solve problems in the future, and we will be the generation leading the shift and bringing real change.

Many headlines seem to focus on the idea that millennials are not poised to lead. We are incompetent, shiftless and noncommittal. We show up late. We act entitled. We demand more than we earn. These generalizations don't change that fact that millions of original millennials are employed and show up to work every single day ready to achieve. These assumptions don't diminish the thousands of problems being solved by original millennials who are revolutionizing the way business is done.

You probably know an original millennial. You may even feel you are one. In this book you will discover how original millennials are influencing key areas of culture. You will meet original millennials who are dispelling the myths and stereotypes of the so-called "Narcissistic" generation. You will find folks like me who knew early in life that they were destined to lead, as I did in 1997. You will discover that original millennials are valuable, loyal, high-performing leaders. You learn lessons of leadership for your life and career. Perhaps most important, you will take away inspiration and hope that the future is in good hands with an original millennial at the helm.

Contents

Introduction
"Original" Millennials Defined

A MILLENNIAL? IS THAT WHAT I'M CALLED?

The debut of CDs and DVDs, the rise of the Internet, the O.J. Simpson trial, the death of Princess Diana, the Columbine shootings, Y2K, the boy band craze, the creation of Napster, terrorism. They all happened when millennials started to emerge. Each event marked a shift in culture that shaped the personality of the millennial generation. If generations had a personality, we could say that the baby boomer generation was shaped by JFK, RFK, MLK, the Vietnam War, rock & roll and Woodstock. We could say that Watergate, the cassette tape, marijuana, HIV, the personal computer, grunge and hip-hop shaped Generation X.

Countless studies have shown how different millennials are than previous generations. With consistent psychographic analysis of our behaviors and our shortcomings, it's understandable how stereotypes about millennials have taken root in society. It's easy to be critical of someone who is perceived to have a different set of ethics and values as you. However, many millennials question how we earned this reputation.

Averaging a reasonable 15-to-16 year timespan, for the purposes of this book we will use the following ranges for each generation:

- Silent Generation (b. 1928-1945)
- Baby Boomer Generation (b. 1946-1964)
- Generation X (b. 1965-1979)
- Generation Y/Millennials (b. 1980-1995)
- Generation Z/Digital Natives (b. 1996 - 2012)

The term millennial applies to individuals who reached adulthood around or after the turn of the 21st century. However, other sources peg different dates to categorize millennials. Neil Howe and William Strauss, authors of the 1991 book, Generations: The History of America's Future, 1584 to 2069, who are credited with coining the term, define the millennial cohort as consisting of individuals born between 1982 and 2004. A major component in their research is showing millennials to be the most affluent and well-educated generation in history.

Some folks will dismiss the name "millennial" altogether because of the labels associated with the generation. Yet there are some millennial personality traits worth considering such as optimistic, patriotic, impatient, entrepreneurial, individualistic yet group oriented, achievement-oriented, financially savvy and wanting instant gratification. Howe and Strauss describe millennials as an ethnically diverse generation of team players that is optimistic, confident, trusting of authority, rule-followers, achievers in school, and generally achievement-oriented in everything they undertake.

WHO ARE MILLENNIALS?

Millennials are known as Generation Y, the demographic cohort that directly follows Generation X. Millennials are the last generation born in the 20th century. Today, there are 1.7 billion millennials comprising one-third of the global population. About 80 million millennials live in the United States, surpassing baby boomers as the largest generation in American history. The millennial has become more ethnically and racially diverse than the previous generation and is also more culturally and racially tolerant than older generations, according to Pew Research.

Millennials comprise the generation that grew up learning technology. We thrive on the connectivity we get from computers, cell phones and the internet because we were introduced to them during our childhood and early teen years. We were somewhat sheltered coddled and slightly coddled by our parents, constantly receiving positive feedback and nurturing in order to build our self-esteem and learn to explore the world for ourselves.

Our interpersonal approach is laid-back, informal and relational. We respect privacy and self-efficacy but will freely share our lives with others. We acknowledge and admire some authorities, but don't mind breaking the rules if it's worth the risk. We'd much rather work to live than live to work because we place a high premium on personal fulfillment. We are often busy, have short attention spans and can adapt well to change. We are free-spirited and open to ideas. We are the generation that gets the most marketing attention from brands but we're the most skeptical of 'in your face' product peddling, and instead place more value on having an authentic experience. We make less money than previous generations, but have the most discretionary income. We've figured out how to use technology to do more and spend less. We love discounts, deals and freebies. We have smaller incomes and bigger debt because we're often underemployed and underpaid. We've put off commitments like marriage and home ownership not because they don't hold value to us but because we want to be stable enough to fully enjoy those experiences without major financial woes. We like money and appreciate the finer things, but live for a bargain. We are patriotic but won't always agree politically. We retreat to music, reality TV or the Starbucks a few blocks away.

MILLENNIAL MANIA

An obsession with millennials has gripped what seems like the entire culture. Millennials are likely the most studied generation to date. Brands and organizations have formed a fascination with how to relate and connect to millennials. Media and scholars have developed a 21st-century style of urgency to understand this demographic. Not since baby boomers has a generation been such a cultural fixation.

According to U.S. Census Bureau statistics, there are plenty of us to study: 80 million plus. Millennials are the largest generation in the U.S. representing one-third of the total U.S. population. We will make up an estimated 50% of the workforce by 2020, ultimately changing the face of organizational leadership.

Not only are millennials the largest generation to date, we are the most traditionally diverse generation in history. A culture shift in the population shows that, among the 80 million millennials and counting, 60% classify as non-Hispanic white, in comparison to 70% of the previous generation. That percentage is projected to continue a decline as ethnic minorities (blacks and hispanics) will account for 60% of the population by 2045.

Among millennials in the U.S., 59% are white and 27% have immigrant backgrounds. The ethnic profile of the millennial is far more blended that than of previous generations, including Hispanic (19%), black (14%), Asian (4%) and mixed race (3%). In addition, there are millennials who come from a growing number of single-parent homes, blended families and families with same sex parents (Broido, 2004.)

This diversity makes millennials the masters of self-expression. Sharing a selfie on a social networking site; posting a live video online; sleeping with a cell phone next to one's bed; donning one or more tattoos or piercings in some place other than an earlobe. They're all part of the millennial way of life. That freedom of expression may drive other generations crazy as decision makers decide how best to market their brands to millennials and organizational leaders express frustration in how to manage us.

For millennials, walking into a room and seeing all types of people is a norm. Diversity of race and gender is a given and in some cases paramount.

Millennials are much more concerned about the diversity of thoughts, ideas and philosophies as we look to understand differences and encourage collaboration.

YOUR MOTHER'S GENERATION

My mom was child of the 60s, born at the end of the Baby Boom. She witnessed black and white television change to color, both literally and figuratively. She watched the death of MLK. She adored The Beatles and The Jackson 5. To her, Michael Jackson wasn't the king of pop. He was a cute kid with a high-pitched voice and an Afro. My mom became a teen of the 70s and adult of the 80s.

Before millennials came along, baby boomers were the largest generation (76 million people worldwide). Born during a spike in childbirths after World War II, boomers currently make up 28% of the U.S population and are the single largest economic group. They grew up during the Civil Rights Movement and the Cold War. The generation that created the term "workaholic," boomers run local, state, and national governments and can be less optimistic, cynical and distrusting of authority figures.

Much like millennials, baby boomers believe rules should be obeyed unless they are contrary to what they want—then it's OK to break them. In their youth, boomers were seen as free-spirited, cause-oriented, experimental and individualistic. They measured their work ethic in hours worked, placing less importance on productivity. A respect for loyalty, rank and relationships is an inherent value for boomers. They are more likely to have married young and had children in the traditional sense of starting a family. Boomers are known to be overprotective of their children, shielding them from life's dangers while giving them just enough freedom and confidence to experience the world on their own. But more and more boomers are "empty nesters" because they've arrived at the age where their children have left home.

The millennial generation's parents are baby boomers and some early born Generation Xers. Most of Generation X's children were born in the mid-to-late 1990s, including millennials and the following generation born in the 2000s. At 50 million people worldwide, Gen X had less of an impact on popular culture until the late 1980s and early 1990s. The "X" described the lack of identity that members of the generation experienced, uncertain of where they belonged in society.

They were first defined as "slackers" before millennials came along and the first generation to develop comfort with technology and to carry a "carpe diem" attitude. Gen X had to learn to fend for themselves as the first latchkey kids since both parents work long hours and has experienced more divorces as children and as spouses than any other generation.

As commonly seen in generational shifts, Gen X is cynical toward things that the previous generation held dear. They are generally proud to not to be the offspring of the baby boom generation and actively rebel against the idealism of the baby boomers with a suspicion of traditional boomer values. While they may reject the idealism of the 1960s, Gen X-ers benefitted from the incubation boomers provided as a safety protecting them from societal problems facing their generation and the millennials as well such as war, protests, violence and discrimination.

Unlike workaholic boomers, Gen X-ers figured out how to work smarter and not harder. They respect open communication regardless of position, title, or tenure. They often have mistrust in institutions and reject the rules, while sometimes still playing it safe to avoid any trouble. They often leap into entrepreneurship later in life as a desire for reinvention and financial flexibility. They value control of their time, seek emotional security and appreciate independent thinking.

We can now understand why there is a great deal of variation from one individual millennial to another, more than within any other generational cohort, when we understand who our parents are. The differences between baby boomer and Gen X-er parents are the most critical reason millennials are so diversely defined yet grossly misunderstood.

As millennials take the lead, all generations must attempt to forge strong intergenerational relationships that deepen their understanding of each other's backgrounds, motivations and perspectives.

WHAT MAKES A MILLENNIAL ORIGINAL

While millennials have a series of subgroups divided by the factors of age and socioeconomic background, we will not refer to those demographics as descriptors for original millennials. It's true that the entrepreneurial members of the older-millennial subset are altogether reinventing the planet and the younger subset is revitalizing organizations with an intrapraneurial excitement that is reinventing the workforce.

A 33-year old millennial remembers using dial-up internet access to log on to the first version of Facebook, while a 23-year old millennial has likely never used Facebook without a high speed mobile or Wi-Fi connection. Those are major moments in the social development of millennials that are not to be ignored. However, the term "original" in this book will not be used to separate millennials by younger and older subsets.

The millennial generation continues to have a major influence on almost every aspect of our lives, including how we communicate and use technology. Millennials have affected changes in parenting practices, educational and career choices and sparked shifts in homeownership and family life. These developments have inspired much speculation about how this generation will fare later in life, and whether these trends are temporary or permanent (TCEA, 2014).

The driving force behind the potential greatness within the millennial generation is originality. We got here with so much originality that we were ready to take on a world that wasn't making room for us.

We get distracted because we switch devices 27 times an hour. It may look like we don't know where we're going with our eyes glued to the screen and our fingers scrolling down the side. But we keep original ideas flowing from the sources found in the platforms we surf.

We thrive on original experiences and relationships. We are cautious and loyal. We often think the media are biased and can quickly perceive fakeness in human interaction.

We must have original conversations that happen in a meaningful, sincere way. We back brands. It gives us a sense of ownership and makes us feel like we contribute to the growth and prominence of those businesses.

We may look up to Mark Zuckerberg, Jay-Z and Steve Jobs for their originality, but our favorite mentors and models for inspiration are our fellow millennials.

Why is this? Because originality can sometimes be at odds with the source. The best parts of original millennials are found in the choice to change and evolve. The original qualities of past generations use commonly understood behavior patterns, which make them far easier to define, whereas original millennials have the ability to defy category.

For the millennial generation, originality is the most important trait because it positions how we think, feel, work and lead. The power of originality becomes most valuable when used in the pursuit of solutions. Millennials always look for ways to make things greater, bigger, better, stronger and more practical.

The purpose of this book is not about pointing out our differences. It's about uplifting a generation by harnessing the original qualities we possess. The distinction of original is applied to the approach millennials bring to life; how we marry vision and values; how we merge creativity with cause and how we make real challenges look remarkably cool. Originality is the prime possession that makes the difference.

Part 1

Career, Entrepreneurship, Intrapreneurship

ALL OF US ARE ENTREPRENEURS

2004. I graduated from college. I'd had four internships while majoring in mass communications. By my senior year one of the internships turned into a part-time job at a local radio station. The work experience made me a top candidate among my peers who were also graduating. I discovered the industry I wanted to work in was public relations. That year, I applied to nearly 100 jobs in the field that best matched my qualifications and landed about 10 interviews. Each company turned me down. I typically got one of two responses, "It came down to you and one other person. We think you're great but we decided to go with the other candidate" or "It seems you're overqualified for this position and we just don't think you'll stay with us long." The job market seemed bleak. No one would hire me. I couldn't determine what the future held. I figured if no one would give me a job I would create my own. I started a business. I decided it would be a public relations firm.

I didn't have any money, not even enough to open a bank account. I didn't know where to get the money I needed for startup costs. My mother bought me a diamond tennis bracelet as a graduation present. I figured it was the highest item of value in my possession. Desperate to become an entrepreneur, I sold it. I took $30 of that money to register for a local business license. I took the rest and paid for a logo, a box of business cards and a website domain. Those were the only things needed to make the business official.

That entrepreneurial spirit I pioneered at 14 years old had kicked in once again and this time I was legit. I started telling fellow grads and former coworkers from the radio station that I had launched a PR firm. They would send me referrals. I began taking meetings and landing client projects. I never took any business classes or worked for a PR firm but I was confident in my ability. I honesty didn't know what I was doing but I researched best practices in PR and vowed to operate with the highest level of integrity. I didn't have much furniture in my one-bedroom apartment so I would stretch out over my air mattress, drag my Compaq desktop to edge and use AOL disks for dial-up internet to look up articles, company profiles and case studies. I would go to the nearest library to print anything that seemed too long to read from a computer monitor. I kept what I had printed in a folder along with my business license.

I assumed people would be wary of my business chops because I was so young. They wouldn't want to pay me because I was inexperienced. Word was spreading and business was steady, but money was slow so I was still applying for full-time jobs in PR (or any entry-level job that paid enough to cover my expenses). Still, no one would hire me. I figured it was a sign to keep growing my business. I always wanted to get a master's degree, so I enrolled in graduate school hoping to add to my credentials and create a cushion to fall back on in case the business didn't take off. I was broke. I was uncertain. I was bold. I was 22. I was a millennial.

THE VALUE OF WORK
By 2020, millennials will represent 50% of the global workplace, making them a huge influence in how business works. Organizational leaders are becoming increasingly concerned that they soon will be unable to find the

talent they need to succeed, with a shortage of suitably skilled workers as the single biggest worry. Businesses are competing fiercely for the best available talent to replace the retiring boomers in the upcoming years. Every year, more and more of that talent will be recruited from the ranks of millennials (PwC, 2011).

That means building leaders from the millennial generation can no longer be a delayed strategy for decision-makers in the workplace.

Reason 1: Millennials are critical to organizational success and sustainability
Reason 2: Millennials can quickly learn the ropes then come for the boss's job
Reason 3: Millennials have options. We can decide we don't want to work for someone
Reason 4: Without millennials, organizations will start to wane.

A report by PriceWaterhouse Coopers provides some insight into the minds of millennials. In 2011, the corporation carried out an online survey of 4,364 millennials across 75 countries under the age of 31 or under and had graduated college between 2008 and 2011. Seventy-five percent were currently employed or about to start a new job while 8% were unemployed at the time they responded to the questionnaire. The rest were self-employed or returning full-time to continue their education. According to the survey, 76% of respondents with a job said it was a graduate role, while 12% had a job that did not require a degree. The survey said that 54% expected to work for between two and five employers over their entire career.

This isn't attributed to low attention spans and bouts of boredom millennials are believed to possess. This is a direct result of organizations determining that millennials aren't high-level contributors because we're not "one-size fits all." We spend an average 1.5 years to 3 years working at a company. But working for two and five employers over a 40 to 50-year career suggests much greater longevity with an employer than that the perceived length of millennials' employment, the survey said.

According to a 2014 survey of 500-plus millennials by "Business Insider" and News To Live By, 16% of millennials don't land a job after graduating from college after searching for six months. Almost a quarter applied to more than 11 full-time jobs before being hired. When they finally got a full-time job, close to half of the respondents found out they didn't a need a college degree to get it.

Jill Jacinto, a millennial expert and associate director for WORKS, a career consultancy, found that many millennials come into the workforce hoping to lock down a secure career and bank on a big payday only to be disappointed that neither of those things were readily available. "There is struggle to find a job and taking anything just to have money," Jill says. "In doing so, it left us frustrated and not being very happy, feeling like we could not live our passion."

Jill knows what she's talking about. She's a millennial, too. Working for a career expert, she has made her living engaging with and representing her generation, but it was her Gen X boss and mentor who showed her how to help people under the generational shift.

Jill started her career as a personal finance reporter. After several years working in journalism she realized she wasn't passionate about EFTs and global trading. She wanted something better. She wanted to find value in her work. She heard business expert Nicole Williams speak at a book-signing event and was blown away by her energy, passion and expertise. She started following her online and reading her books.

Shortly after, a friend forwarded her an email of a job opening with Nicole's company. Jill met with Nicole about the position. She didn't get that job, but did get the nod for a newly created role that Nicole had in mind. Since Nicole was a go-to expert in coaching and consulting for businesses and executives, she noticed a need to help clients better understand the value of work for the millennial generation. She selected Jill to begin speaking at conferences, writing articles, producing video segments and events. She began working with corporations and advising Fortune 500 companies on recruiting and marketing to millennials for a better understanding of the generation. With her background in journalism and media, she was a perfect fit to talk, write and advise companies about millennials.

Jill soon became a millennial expert for AOL Jobs and the millennial ambassador for Bentley's PreparedU Project. She has appeared on Fox & Friends and her advice has appeared in Yahoo! Finance, Fox Business, Bloomberg Radio, MSN Money, Refinery 29, Reuters, Business Insider, Huffington Post & Cosmo for Latinas.

"I had a boss who believed in my potential," she says. "Even though she was an expert, she wasn't a millennial but she knew that clients needed help understanding millennials for their organizations. She made me feel confident and capable in representing my generation. She also empowered me to do what I was good at and helped me grow. Those are the kinds of things that millennials value most in their work."

Organizations are learning that in order to attract and retain millennial talent, they must use a more non-traditional approach to job creation and satisfaction. They must match our job skills and career goals with their business needs and key objectives. This is how we find value in our work.

Sitting at a cluttered cubicle for eight hours or more is not what we have in mind. We are less concerned with job roles, titles and duties and place more emphasis on bringing value to our lives through our work. We also tend to be uncomfortable with rigid corporate structures and are turned off by business silos that isolate team members from one another.

We expect rapid progression once our true talents are revealed to those we report to. We want a varied and interesting career and need consistent feedback. We need a management style and corporate culture that meets our professional and personal needs. But some organizations are reluctant to provide for the values their millennial employers demand.

Why?

Jill says it is because they are afraid to accept that the cultural shift to millennials in leadership is happening faster than expected. Early on, organizations knew our generation was different and resisted the change until it started impacting the growth of business. "When the word 'millennials' first came into the vernacular of the workplace, many organizations were asking what it meant," Jill says. " The word was attached to a negative connotation of a selfish me-generation."

She believes it takes a lot of effort from our generation to change people's preconceived notions on who millennials are and what we do in the workspace. "Millennials are just another generation dealing with different types of adversity, relating to life by using technology, adapting to life's changes, and disrupting the traditional workspace," Jill says. "We are going to have to change the perception by being respectful and thoughtful leaders for the organizations in which we work."

Millennials are vocal about what we want for our lives. Our careers are top priority. In fact, our generation sees a bigger picture for our work, leveraged by technology, freedom and creativity. This means we have the ability to add meaningful value to our work from anywhere at anytime, and we must be allowed to exercise that value in ways that others respect it.

There are some important challenges that have impacted how we value work. Because our generation has less work experience and more tenuous connections to employers than older workers, we are often let go from organizations in greater numbers and have to compete against more experienced workers for new jobs once recovery begins. We therefore tend to be among the last groups to recover fully from the devastation wrought by economic recession and mass layoffs (TCEA, 2014).

Jill admits the challenges have made the search for the true value of our work a difficult one. "Our generation grew up reading headline after headline announcing the latest corporate scandal so understandably we are skeptical of big business," she says. "We watched our parents work for years and years at the same company and believe they had a nest egg for retirement that somehow disappeared. Millennials did not want to follow in our parents' footsteps. We started scrambling up extra money in addition to our full time job as side hustles."

Since we have witnessed instability in the workplace, wild business scandals on the news involving heralded corporate leaders and the downsizing of our parents' jobs after they committed loyal years of service, we have developed certain perceptions regarding the value of work that organizations may overlook.

The connection between millennials and the corporate workplace is joined by stereotypes. While we are pegged as a less valuable demographic in the world of work, organizations forget what sketchy and distrustful conditions we've been exposed to. These factors and more impact unemployment rates, which among millennials is almost twice that of all previous generations of workers, and reveal how many of us are actually underemployed (meaning being overqualified in our current position or being paid less than we should with more bills than income).

"We are constantly told growing up to avoid risks at all costs when it came to our work," Jill says. " You must have stability and security so stay on the traditional path at all costs and you will find success and fulfillment in that, when in reality, the world no longer worked that way."

Millennials do not want to put their passion on hold, however. We forego the wait by working jobs that can provide some level of satisfaction and start businesses on the side that fuel our deeper interests. Jill advises millennials to find a career that combines passion with skill and to create open communication with employers that allows them to understand your professional goals. "Initially you may be scared to take those first few steps in your career by having open discussions with your employers or take an idea you are inspired by then creating a side business from it," she says. "But the millennials who are doing that are more successful and optimistic about their world of work and present themselves as having higher value because they are in control of their careers and decide to bravely face those professional challenges head on."

The main challenge for establishing value in the workplace can be gradually addressed when millennials and employers make an attempt to connect and communicate better. "The idea that millennials are more likely to jump ship or become disengaged if a job doesn't fulfill our passion could be partly true, however we mainly move on or disconnect when it seems a job doesn't match our aspirations," Jill adds. "That's when we use one of our greatest attributes: we speak up. Millennials are prepared to ask for what we want more than any other generation of workers but our needs and wants are no different."

Millennials can show employers we're loyal by expressing our need for professional growth and retention within our organizations. Our place in the cultural shift has uniquely prepared us to translate technological complexities and help demonstrate how pushing past discomfort can result in greater ease and efficiency.

When we define and prove our value, we create leverage to ask for more of what we want. 🐦 @theOGmillennial

Ask your employer for the resources to pursue education in your chosen field and opportunities to keep learning through training, workshops or tuition reimbursement. Also, be prepared to invest in your own training outside of the office to make your skills as marketable and transferable as possible. Ask for time with your manager for an explanation for how your specific contributions add to the company's bottom line and how the team benefits from the efficiencies you can create.

Ask if you can mentor fellow millennials in the workplace who may need to be coached on the company's culture. Offer to be a reverse mentor to baby boomers or Gen X-ers as an effort to build relationships with senior colleagues that could raise the bar on employee engagement and productivity. If you seek leadership in the workplace, ask for an honest assessment of your communication weaknesses and make sure you are working to inspire confidence, showing interest in the professional development of your coworkers and communicating with clarity and transparency.

Tweet: Be curious about what's going on in the world. @jilljacinto #theOGmillennial

THE VARIETY OF INTRAPRENEURSHIP

Increasingly passionate millennials are wrapping the boredom and underwhelm of their full time jobs around their own innovative and visionary agendas. While organizations find value in a plethora of traits, business ownership and entrepreneurial education has become a major plus on an applicant's resume. In a time where organizations are experiencing difficulty finding millennials who have the skills to become leaders, they are learning to have a greater appreciation for the variety of nontraditional experiences that place millennials in leadership roles making critical decisions.

Seventy-one percent of millennials already consider themselves to be leaders, even though less than half hold formal leadership positions, according to a survey of 527 millennial professionals (ages 18-35) conducted by Virtuali, a leadership training company.

A national Millennial Mindset Study of 1,200 employed millennials conducted by online training platform Mindflash revealed that a "lack of company support for training and development" is the most surprising aspect of work in the "real world." This reality likely contributes to the fact that an overwhelming majority (88%) of millennials are willing to invest personally or sacrifice anything—from vacations to coffee habits—to train themselves in the skills needed to compete in the workforce today.

Many millennials are already putting this commitment into action. According to Mindflash, 31% of the employed 18-33 year-old Americans who took part in the study—most of whom have at least seven years of work experience—report that while it is tough to keep up with the skills they need to do their job, they seek out training on their own to fill the gaps.

Organizations acknowledge they have done a poor job of providing training for leadership skills, so they are relieved when millennials bring those practical qualities to the table - no matter where or how the experience was earned. Millennials are taking the lead on project teams, volunteering their expertise and influencing people toward achievement. Serving as the chair or host of a local networking event, starting an online business with a few friends, leading a team of people for a volunteer project, building a crowdfunding campaign for a startup; these are the sort of leadership experiences that demonstrate to employers that you have what is called an "intrapreneurial" spirit.

Intrapreneurship is the practice of entrepreneurial development of a new idea, process, or service within the environment of an established organization. For millennials, it has become a critical means to making authentic contributions and birthing ideas that position us as leaders.

The development has ushered in a significant shift in corporate culture, in which millennials of any age can be seen as thought leaders by their employers.

Employers have begun to recognize the misconception that millennials don't have built-in leadership skills. Some millennials may have acquired a variety of leadership skills in their college activities and internship duties, and maybe even sports teams or side hustles, but a good chunk of our generation has not. Without leadership training, millennials can still make their way forward.

Meanwhile, employers often have a disdain for spending money, time and effort to conduct training and invest resources for fear that the millennial employee will take their skill sets to another company. In turn, they cheat the millennial employee and the company by withholding access to beneficial knowledge that could support the intrapraneurial spirit among millennials and yield a strong return on investment for the company.

Millennials in companies of all sizes are using intrapreneurship to keep their organizations up to date while their leaders are noticing how intrapreneurship ignites innovation and helps retain the best talent within their ranks. For instance, millennials shine as intrapreneurs when we show our organizations how to save money on a particular process by using technology, integrate social media into a communication function and create a widget that increases workplace productivity and efficiency. We also show our intrapreneurial instinct when we establish a program that introduces the company as an industry leader to a new target audience or develop a community partnership that connects to the company's corporate social responsibility program.

Jill sees how organizations flourish from the millennial intrapreneur who works inside a major corporation and decides to develop and promote solutions to social or environmental challenges in an area of the business where progress has stalled. "The millennial generation is one of incredible resilience and creativity," Jill says. "We've looked at the challenges of cultural change in ways that other generations have not and we often seek new methods of tackling areas in which organizations feel stuck, undecided or uncertain. We like having an insider-outsider mindset and applying an entrepreneurial approach to the problems inside our organizations."

As an example of how millennials are starting to influence the organizations where they work, take Deloitte's "Wicked Problems," a crowdsourcing initiative that taps the collective intelligence of professionals throughout the world. Deloitte used Wicked Problems to ask all its employees questions such as "What's important to you?" and "How can we engage in what's important to you?" Deloitte also organizes innovation-on-demand forums, including labs and cafes, that foster time for employees to talk, listen, reflect, evaluate and ideate.

The intrapreneurship of millennials is our way of demanding our own leadership development, creating our own learning outcomes and adding variety to our own careers. Understanding that the power of intrapreneurship is a vital ingredient in maintaining an edge as a millennial in leadership becomes the key source for the variety we desire. As the biggest generation in U.S. history, we can be a force for the implementation of workplace innovation, growth and flexibility.

Not only are we more optimistic than older generations and always seek to increase the variety in our careers, we see our work as one aspect of a fully integrated life. We are well aware of the internal bureaucracy in larger companies, as frustration with old methods of doing business lead to more turnover among millennials. Therefore, once you become familiar with your organization's culture and discover its attached to a few old processes, be prepared to replace them with recommendations for new ideas to implement. Try to identify at least one process that can remain, but be improved on for better results.

We are the masters of multitasking. We are great at juggling multiple tasks and responsibilities. It's a result of our need for variety. The challenge for millennials is that multitasking can create a lack of engagement and limit the traditional elements found in business interactions. A successful intrapreneur recognizes the balance between going hard on everything and going human with everyone, so that interactions are developed and not ignored.

We are able to create solutions that aren't expensive or difficult to implement but require management to shift its thinking about how its been approaching the function. Within an organizational structure, it takes time for new concepts to move out of their traditional boxes, for teams to strategize a different road map and for employees to advocate for change. As millennials become a significant majority of the workforce and capture key leadership positions, we must insist on leadership that looks like intrapraneurship. We have a head start. Let's keep fueling our desire to challenge conventional thinking and ignite action around intrapraneurship.

Ask management for leadership and personality assessments to better understand your traits as an intrapreneurial leader. Seek a professional coach and internal mentors who can advise you along the way. We are comfortable with transparency and want management to practice it as they are grooming us. We get the basic ingredients for success, but can gain valuable guidance as the benefit of some unconventional advice. Be prepared to make improvements along the way based on the feedback you receive. And, don't be offended, even if you don't agree with what comes out of the evaluation. Use it to your advantage. When we ask management to help us, we should reciprocate a tone of clarity and openness, with a respect for inclusion and diversity.

We know that all of us won't own businesses. Wearing the title of business owner may be something many millennials won't do. It doesn't mean we are not all entrepreneurial. We are all entrepreneurs. We just foster the entrepreneurial spirit through different channels and avenues. While many millennials are causing market disruption through their startup businesses, corporate intrapreneurs are gaining prominence by helping legacy companies prepare for the digital future.

Intrapraneurial millennials are reinventing the workplace through corporate experiences. We should expect organizations to reward this kind of creative thinking instead of marginalizing it. The implications for corporate innovation are daunting. It's one thing for companies to track their competitors through normal methods, and another for companies to identify, nurture and invest in millennial talent that can eagerly stay on a competitors' tracks. Too often companies become stagnate by avoiding discussions about new developments. Then, all of sudden, they get hit with a disruption of the next big thing that changes how they fundamentally operate. When intrapreneurial millennials take the lead, it doesn't have to be that way. When we take the lead, we identify the trends that are shaping the future and take action to shape it before others shape it for us.

The age of the intrapreneur has begun. Given the opportunity to create your own career, you may find that the one offered by your employer lacks variety. Major parts of your job may seem dull and unfulfilling. However, the millennials who rise to leadership are the ones who are energetic, full of ideas for innovation and embrace change. During the next wave of millennial work, we must use our collective power to seek workplace change as intrapraners.

THE VISION FOR ENTREPRENEURSHIP
If you ask someone to describe the term "entrepreneur," she will probably tell you that it is someone who starts a business. She will probably throw out words like "visionary," "risk-taker," "hustler" or "leader." Ask her to

describe a few characteristics of an entrepreneur and you will hear "aggressive," or "influential." You may envision someone running a startup in her basement while wearing pajamas or someone jet-setting and transacting big deals. Perhaps you picture a person with six months salary in the bank and a plan to transition from full time employee to small business owner. Or maybe you envision someone who fills his nights and weekends flipping his side hustle into a future Fortune 500 company. Each guess is correct. They all fit the profile of an entrepreneur.

Small business has become one of the largest drivers of the U.S. economy, providing jobs for the nation's private workforce. Millennial entrepreneurs have become essential to job creation in the U.S. In 2011, millennials launched nearly 160,000 startups each month while 25% of all U.S. entrepreneurs were 20 to 34 years old, according to the National Chamber of Foundation. Meantime, 72% of millennials would like to be their own boss. 27% are already self-employed. Males, blacks and Latinos are most inclined to start their own business while females are more likely start nonprofits.

We're reminded of the work of the millennial entrepreneur everyday. Do you know how Snapchat began? It was created as a class project at Stanford University. How about Tinder? The result of a childhood partnership that reconnected by technology at USC. And what about Twitter? Well, its founder, Jack Dorsey, was an undergrad at NYU when he developed his idea that would change the world. And, of course, we know the all too-familiar tale of Facebook, created by Harvard student Mark Zuckerberg. The innovators responsible for the most recent advancements in technology and social media are getting younger and younger. Now, more than 2,100 U.S. colleges and universities have added the study of entrepreneurship as a major or minor (National Chamber Foundation, 2012).

The millennial generation, more than previous generations, has faced increased competition for the best jobs, so much so that we in many cases we're underemployed. Many us are either unemployed, inadequately employed or dropped out of the labor market altogether. It's no wonder we're becoming our own bosses. The overall unemployment rate for millennials between ages 18 to 34 peaked being more than 13 percent in 2010, the latest year for which figures are available, also led many millennials to become entrepreneurs. The entrepreneurial mindset among millennials could actually support the economic recovery and sustain small business, helping to reverse a declining trend of startups that are here today and gone tomorrow.

But we face obstacles. The ability to get a loan or credit is the biggest challenge for starting a business, along with the lack of education and resources to run a small business. Although there are tons of programs for startups that will coach, incubate and mentor small businesses through the early phases to make them sustainable, many millennials choose to wing it and learn the ropes for as long as possible without turning to help. The uncertainty of what to do and where to turn could have a negative impact on the viability of our businesses and create a longer trek to real growth. However, because starting a business in today's digital age is cheaper and less risky, millennials can prove to be the most seasoned, experienced generation of entrepreneurial leaders yet.

Joe Holberg is one millennial entrepreneur who knows the impact of financial obstacles. He had to borrow $40 from a neighbor to pay for his college application. Coming up with the next $40,000 in tuition was going to be tough. While at the University of Michigan, he had to work extremely hard to earn a B.S. in Economics while juggling multiple jobs along the way. It wasn't easy making ends meet. After his sophomore year, Joe ran out of money and finished with grants. With these hardships in mind, instead of joining corporate America, Joe decided to join AmeriCorps to work with entrepreneurs and low-income families. "I knew I wanted to be the kind of entrepreneur who helped people manage their finances but I had to begin by being very strategic," Joe says.

Realizing that there was a lot work to do in the community, he joined Teach For America and began teaching math on the west side of Chicago. He had become increasingly passionate about educating young people about money that he infused lessons on finance into his math class. His students loved it. After a fellowship at Google, Joe built CS First, a technology program that has impacted more than 100,000 students globally. He then received a grant from Google to teach coding for an underrepresented group of minorities, girls and underserved kids in South Carolina and provide the students with Chromebooks. Joe taught himself how to code and ending up taking the program across the country for two years. Still a young millennial, Joe soon began advising families how to manage their finances and file their taxes and teaching business and finance classes for adults. Each experience added more fuel to Joe's entrepreneurial fire. He realized it was time to take leap into entrepreneurship and start a company that helped people make and manage their money, with a specific focus on financial planning for the millennial generation.

"I had to learn, in my early days, how to handle complex and often confusing information alone and it shouldn't be an isolating feeling," Joe says. "I believe that everyone should be able to find the support and answers they need about their financial situation, to avoid costly mistakes and create financially comfortable future. So I designed my company to help millennials can take control of their finances and ultimately reach their dreams."

His company, Holberg Financial, conducts tax prep, financial coaching and financial planning for millennials. It also helps low-income families avoid exploitation from companies who may be all about making the dollar instead of making a difference. "The idea that when you're low-income, lack certain resources or come from a younger generation you have a different set of issues is somewhat of a myth," Joe says. "We all have the same needs and wants—financial security, family stability, retirement savings. That's why entrepreneurship is important. It gives us an additional streams of income if we do it as a supplement, in addition to our jobs, or it has the possibility of creating a generational wealth for a lifetime if it's our only career focus."

As millennials age, many factors will bear down on our financial future: Social Security is underfunded, our life expectancy is on the rise and college debt won't disappear. While Joe was working with older generations prior to starting his business, he was often challenged with the pressure to perform knowing that he only had certain amount of time to improve the wealth of his older clients. He's concerned that millennials, especially those who are entrepreneurial, don't always learn things we should about money or by the time we do we've already been cast out into the world and are burdened by money mistakes and financial mess-ups. "Most businesses are not established to make money," Joe says. "They are started for a higher purpose of service. If you begin right and manage wisely, the money follows. However, millennials are a considerably underfinanced generation, which is why we have no choice but to start living on significantly less and start our own businesses."

The decision to start a business is one of the first steps in the entrepreneurial process, involving ideation around problem-solving, significant commitments of time and financial resources. There's also a great deal of risk and uncertainty involved in the decision to start your own business.

Being an entrepreneur usually means you work when, where and how you like as long as you are delivering results. Being an entrepreneur offers freedom, flexibility and gives life to the notion of "work-life balance." Being an entrepreneur is a lifestyle, not a job. And, being an entrepreneur is anything but easy, though we still see millennials making their own way in the world as entrepreneurs.

Rather than work for companies, we work for ourselves. It is anticipated that 30% or more of millennials will hold various positions as

freelancers and contractors, a way of fending for ourselves and not serving any one particular master. And often, those of us who are able to create their own space in business and find success are typically crazy talented with just the kind of stuff needed to take on leadership roles in corporations. Meanwhile, those corporations are responding to the presence of startups by becoming more like startups and competing with them at their own game.

Our generation approaches entrepreneurship as a way of life. As millennials, we are making decisions on future employment. We have to build self-efficacy to learn entrepreneurship. "The cultural shift with our generation introduces a different formula for millennials who are becoming entrepreneurs," Joe says. "The new equation is to go to school and pursue something you value then make change in that area and go pursue something else and make change in that area. The idea of entrepreneurship is to keep that cycle going."

Ask yourself, "Can I do the same work I perform on my job within my own business as an entrepreneur?" If the answer is yes, consider building a vision of striking out on your own. If that seems too unsettling, consider building a vision of working with partner or pursuing another area of interest as your entrepreneurial venture. Sometimes we run the risk of oversimplifying the work of an entrepreneur by glamorizing the lifestyle. This oversimplification makes us assume growth happens overnight and that challenges of change are slow and easy to adjust to. Not so. Entrepreneurship is a grind with plenty of demands but just enough rewards for the vision to take shape and pay off.

Know your industry and company's purpose. Know the goals and benchmarks that measure your entrepreneurial success. Know how your business makes the world a better place. If you can't connect those dots, reframe your vision of entrepreneurship.

To gain further clarity on your entrepreneurial vision, ask and answer:

- What is the main problem my business solves?
- How do my services/products generate revenue?
- What is the best way to reach my target audience?
- How will I develop a plan to grow my business and make it sustainable?

Look for organizations that offer resources for entrepreneurs running start-ups such as incubator space, angel investments, business coaches, development centers or venture capital programs. These resources provide new ventures with focus, credibility, networks, experience and expertise. Know enough to know you don't know enough. You will need people to help you along with the way. You will learn lessons, fail often and win big, it's all part of the cycle that entrepreneurs go through. Information and education is needed for all of us to cultivate our vision for entrepreneurship.

Know the difference between an entrepreneur and small business owner. An entrepreneur is someone who owns a small business. A small business owner is an entrepreneur who owns a small business he runs with the help of employees, contractors or interns. Both can be self-employed or work as an extra gig, and both can be financially lucrative. Managing a small business can present different challenges or require different emphases compared with the startup of a new entrepreneurial venture. To prepare for these challenges, you must commit to acquiring new skills and knowledge at each level of growth.

Plan for your finances to keep you comfortable. As you go into entre-preneurship, you may start off with a bit of capital or investments but it can take a while for the cash register to start ringing. You will have highs and lows. Have a vision for where you might want the business to be financially. Create a budget to determine how much revenue you need to generate, how much profit should you pocket for living expenses and how much of your business costs can be kept on the low end. If you need financial advice, just ask Joe.

Millennials are not interested in purposeless work. We are not lazy. We don't think the world owes us. We just want more out of life and want to leave the world a better place than before we arrived. As we manage our entrepreneurial efforts—effectively aligned with our vision for being leaders—we must focus on outcomes, not hours, and results, not hype. We must have the vision to create a business culture that expresses sincere care and concern for the business success and overall wellbeing of our customers and our employees. We must have the vision to connect with fellow millennial entrepreneurs through shared purpose of leadership in order to experience greater customer engagement and community involvement. For millennial entrepreneurs to grow our businesses, we must apply compelling vision. It's about principle above all.

Entrepreneurship is a world-changing job centered on your vision. Build a business that's a unique expression of who you are and stands out in a crowded marketplace. Translate your vision into real work that connects with and inspires others, and make your work an authentic reflection of yourself by creatively using limited resources.

The predictable and exponential growth of the millennial entrepreneur is based on a vision for the future because rapid developments in the culture and the economy are simply what we've always experienced. For those with low interest in spending the years climbing the corporate ladder, this transformation will be quite beneficial and require great vision. Combined with our ability to invoke out-of-the-box thinking and engage with people from all walks of life, it's incredibly critical for millennials not only to pursue entrepreneurship, but more easily use our entrepreneurial gifts to disrupt the next product, service or industry.

Tweet: Entrepreneurship gives us the confidence to pursue the unknown. @holberg #theOGmillennial

LESSON #1: ALL OF US ARE ENTREPRENEURS.

We are all born with the innate ability to survive; and survival involves innovative thinking. Think about your life. Think about the things you've seen in your community that bother you. Think about the times you needed to make a decision—a choice—that involved doing something you were not accustomed to doing, but were motivated by the challenge.

You are ready for the world. You are already well adapted to technology. You have a better grasp of the now, and can more easily navigate the next steps to tomorrow. Have you identified your entrepreneurial spirit and allowed it to flourish?

As millennials—no matter our age, race, education, background or financial status—we place a frame of awareness around our lives that presents our communities signified of great importance, our lifestyle as low maintenance; our self-worth detached from the constraints of a job and our wellbeing as complete quality. It's only natural that we are the generation that is making everyone else reconsider they want their legacies to be.

Part 2

Problem Solving, Disruption, Innovation

SEEK TO SOLVE A PROBLEM

2007. I ran out of money. I unexpectedly lost three of my largest accounts. It started with a client that was losing revenue and admitted they could no longer afford my services. Then suddenly another client confessed they had overspent on big events and business trips and needed to cut back. About a week later, another client informed me that they would not be renewing their contract and decided to go a different direction with their PR strategy. I still had a few small accounts but the total revenue wasn't enough to cover my monthly expenses. This all happened within one month. It was the beginning of the Great Recession and I wasn't paying attention. I could say I saw it coming but I honestly didn't. I had a sense that I needed to be going after more clients, increasing the revenue of my business and saving up my money but I wasn't prepared to lose any of my current clients. I was having fun with being a young entrepreneur. I was traveling and partying. I had gotten lost in perks of my profession. Overall, my business had been successful but now I was afraid. Before I knew it, my brand new car had been repossessed, my rent was behind, and my deferred student loans from grad school were about to start repayment. I had no more money and no one to ask for help.

I always liked solving problems. In rare moments have I been afraid of challenges. Since I was a kid, I found so much energy from seeing an obstacle become an opportunity. Challenges always seemed to excite me. I was a trouble-shooter who liked to get to the bottom of things. I was a fixer by nature and by profession. Facing problems and solving them had never been a real issue for me until now. I needed to figure this out.

I was convinced that this problem was an opportunity to reevaluate the approach I had taken to entrepreneurship. I needed to start thinking with more innovation. What could I do solve my money problems? How could I use my talents to disrupt my space in business by presenting some new ideas? What new problems do my potential clients have? What services could they now afford? I developed a plan to establish multiple streams of income. I assessed what the new need was in the current market. I restructured the pricing structure for my client fees. I revamped the services my business offered. I added social media consulting as a service for small businesses and non-profits. I advised formerly employed professionals who were now entrepreneurs due to job loss how to enhance and develop their personal brand. I created a blog as a platform to write about my areas of expertise and increase the visibility of my personal brand. On top of all that, I got a full-time job in my field with a plan to stay long enough to get my budget back on track and used any profits from my business for savings. I literally hustled my way back to financial security.

I was broke, again. I was disruptive. I was repositioning. I was innovative. I was a 25. I was a millennial.

WHAT'S YOUR PROBLEM?

A burning question. A lingering dilemma. A broken system. A person who is hurting. Each qualify as a problem, waiting for someone's attention. A problem is a situation with a set of circumstances needing to be addressed. For example, a situation for a healthcare provider might be the availability of physicians and medical personnel needed to provide care to a growing population of underserved patients. For a small, nonprofit organization dealing with at-risk youth, a situation might be the misunderstanding of how to communicate and meet the immediate needs of youths pressured to join a local gang.

A problem derives from situation that can be viewed as an obstacle that needs to be overcome or an opportunity that should be taken advantage of. A situation identified as an opportunity is something to be embraced because of the positive advantage it may offer. On the other hand, a situation may be an obstacle to overcome because it limits the potential for success and increases the likelihood for disappointment.

Jihan Spearman has had her share of both kinds of situations. She is a millennial practicing law in San Francisco and managing regulatory compliance for mobile devices and innovative technologies at a multinational financial institution.

Growing up, she would watch the TV show "Beverly Hills 90210" and notice that the kids whose fathers were attorneys seemed to be well off. She dreamed of that lifestyle, not because of fancy houses, cars or clothes, but because those families didn't have any worries.

Jihan grew up with a variety of financial struggles, and although it seemed like an outlandish dream to become an attorney, it made her feel empowered to choose a career in which she had expert knowledge of government laws and could defend others when they faced life's problems. She often felt pushed around alongside her immigrant mother who was not used to the U.S. systems, lacked understanding of the processes in government and didn't have anyone to advocate for her. She didn't have the power to speak up on things that were done wrongly and unjust. So one of the best ways for her to cultivate her voice as a leader aiming to help the underserved and disadvantaged was to become an attorney.

"One of the building blocks to being a great leader is learning how to solve problems," she says. "As millennials, we often have generational baggage or cultural burdens that cripple us and make us feel unworthy to reap the benefits of overcoming our problems. It was important for me to decide that I would channel the feeling of helplessness into helping people solve their problems in everyday life, as an advocate during their most troubling times."

One obstacle millennials face in achieving success is the perception that many of us struggle with everyday problem solving—a perpetual indecisiveness that makes us needy and unoriginal. Whether it's the young auditor who texts his boss with every little detail rather than prepare a reasoned explanation for tax exceptions or the tech support rep who keeps repeating stock answers even though he didn't address the customer's true needs, there's a belief that millennials just don't know how to handle problems.

Problem solving is a process for moving a situation from an undesirable to a more desirable condition. We can create different processes for solving problems and develop different interpretations of how people come to decisions. When addressing problems, you must assess the issue at hand. You must consider the source of the problem and present multiple options for solutions. Solutions are what matters most. If you are focusing on the problem, you have it wrong.🐦 @theOGmillennial

"One of the reasons I've been able to achieve success is due to the way I learned how to look at problems at a very young age," Jihan says. "I looked at the things that bothered me and figured out how to make them work. I realized that coming up with grandiose ideas was okay as long as I stayed focused on creating the result and gave less energy to the problem. Millennials must believe that the solutions we come up with are achievable and worthy."

Like many millennials, Jihan was riddled with a student loan at high interest rates and had to make her paying down her debt down a top priority. In many cases, we seek outside pursuits to make extra cash but also to balance our desires to have an impact in areas other than the workplace. Most millennials enhance their ability to effectively solve problems on the job, but more than anything, we use it to figure out how to progress financially.

With the requirement to solve the problems as both obstacles and opportunities, we end up with "slash" careers. Slashes are for people who pursue multiple careers or vocations simultaneously. Millennials have taken the notion of moonlighting and turned it on its head. That means that when it comes to solving problems, we get hyped. We turn out to be resourceful. We become adaptable and engaged.

For Jihan, working as an emerging leader in a large multinational organization enables her to take care of those problems. It's a bonus that she actually enjoys her job. It gives her financial security but allows her the time to add a few slashes as she engages in other entrepreneurial projects. "I love that my current job affords me the ability to earn a great income," she says, "but it doesn't give me the opportunity to reach and mentor millennials who are seeking to solve problems in the world just like I was."

Jihan's first slash is as a consultant using her legal background to help tech start-ups solve problems in creative and ethical ways. Her second slash is as board member of a women's rights law firm that does impactful work across the country. For the third slash, Jihan is founder of Spear Career, a career advice blog for millennials. She noticed an opportunity to speak to millennials who were following fashion and career blogs. Jihan decided to meld millennials and a career in fashion to inform the content of her blog. She uses the site to explore a wide variety of topics geared toward millennials, especially women.

"Unlike the stereotypes, so many millennials are working around the clock wearing multiples hats and making things happen," Jihan says. "We may spread ourselves thin adding slash after slash, but we should find these chances to lead to be immensely valuable exercises in problem solving."

As millennials become a larger percentage of the workforce, we are embracing the shift to address issues in business and community as an opportunity for leadership and service. Organizations that don't follow this shift will lose their appeal and ability to attract millennial talent.

As millennials morph into multi-faceted leaders, we become more and more valuable to the greater community and able to maneuver in what is an increasingly fluid economy.

Identify the problem in the world about which you want to solve. What part of your situation are you trying to change? Is a systemic situation with many cultural factors and social forces keeping the problem in place? Is it an immediate situation that's a simple reaction to supply and demand?

Generate ideas to solve the problem by capturing the opportunity or defeating the obstacle. Assess and assemble the necessary resources. What research can help identify the situation appropriately? What approach do you want to take toward a solution? What methods, people and tools make the most sense to employ?

Implement your solutions and monitor the results to test how well they work in practice. How will you capture the results? How do they fit into your life and impact those around you? How much time and attention must you invest to maintain the results? If you didn't solve the problem, how can you refine or repeat the process until you meet your desired goals?

Millennials need to know the answers to these and so many other questions. We are curious problem solvers who need to know why precise procedures are in place. We want to know why a distinct strategic solution is implemented and why policies are structured in a certain fashion. Why? Because clear explanations reveal the thought process behind leadership decisions and create knowledge-sharing opportunities.

When preparing for leadership, make sure you've asked the right questions. Ask why your company's organizational chart wears a specific structure and why the path to leadership looks the way it does. This will help you get an idea of how to approach problems based on what you've learned about an organization and its culture. Rather than sinking into repetition at work and at home, ask yourself what else can you give to the communities around you. Asking questions gives millennials deeper insight into the problem solving process.

Own the solution. Millennials like ownership. We love the ability to say, "I led that project," or "That's my campaign," but we should seek to solve problems with that same enthusiasm. The assumption is that whoever owns the problem has to solve it. Not so. We have to avoid admiring the problem—talking about it over and over; how intimidating it looks, how complex it seems—and just jump in and try to solve it.

You are probably solving a problem right now simply by taking ownership and moving the process towards a solution. Rather than focus on the problem, focus on owning the solution. The millennial who immediately starts focusing on solving a problem versus someone grumbling over the root cause is one who will be the most valued.

Remember, millennials have entered the workplace as the largest, most ethnically and socially diverse generation to date and are the first generation of digital natives. Ownership for us can lead to solving major issues in the world surrounding cultural awareness and information innovation.

THE POINT OF DISRUPTION

Millennials have a special gift for figuring out what's next. However, the exceptionally important challenges we face require a fire in the belly. Jihan had a coach who inspired her to locate the fire in her belly; an extra inner drive to be an agent of change. It's not just an expression; it's an undeniable desire to affect change at all costs that's felt deep in your gut.

Disruption is defined as the interruption of a process or event. It can be destructive or it can be constructive. It is at the intersection of "This is how it's always been done" and "Let's try something new." It's the thing that causes revolution of thought. It's a freshness of thinking that creates change.

Disruption causes adversity in subtle and incremental ways. We tend to think of disruption as the major events in our lives that cause adversity such as the loss of a family member or job, an illness or accident, a bankruptcy or foreclosure.

However, adversity can gradually unravel our lives. It can be the start of the disruption to the life we know. As millennials, the mere presence of our generation presented a disruption in society that introduced adversity for us, such as the criticism of our values, manners and behaviors. In turn, we respond with our own kind of disruption, the kind that shifts society's perception to view us as leaders.

Jihan is a multicultural, multi-ethnic woman in a conservative, bureaucratic, highly regulated environment, working to gain respect from older generations. But, to millennials, ideas matter most. Culturally, we are in space where disruption with new and innovative ideas is rewarded.

"I made the job I was hired to do more efficient and developed innovative ways to minimize and avoid risks, mitigate loss, and improve controls across the departments," Jihan said. "Many of the solutions I've created rival a lot of the people who've been at the company for a long time. And even though I find myself constantly outperforming others to proof my worth and gain respect, which can be tiring at times, I feel disruption is the only way to bridge the gap."

Overcoming adversity in her childhood organically gave Jihan a disruptive mindset. Daily life required disrupting the norm by finding a new and innovative approach for survival. Experiencing points of frustration and discomfort made her strive to figure out why things are the way they are and how to fix them.

"Millennials are a curious generation that demanded a drastic change in the way information was presented. We have benefitted from the spread of technology and in turn, we have been able disrupt industries by taking knowledge into our communities and helping others advance their skills without having to go into debt and do it in shorter periods of time," Jihan adds. "Disruption has created a shift from the value of education to the value of innovation. And, while education has been a pillar of support for me, I understand that the value system has shifted because of our courage to disrupt the norm."

As millennials, we've seen how high values and expectations can inspire the process of disruption. Without disruption, we cannot close the generational loop and establish lasting engagement around issues in leadership. We cannot develop bonds of loyalty with brands, organizations and communities if we are afraid of shifting the norm. Millennial leaders using disruption as a cultural element of change means that we lead with intention. We need to clearly articulate the importance of—and commitment—to disruption.

To use disruption effectively, you must first be knowledgeable about the space you are trying to impact. The same is true of the entrepreneurial space. To build a successful company, you need to first understand the different aspects of your industry and respect its current state. Disruption will not be the answer to every problem. Things don't have to be broken in order for them to be improved.

Some processes simply need to be adjusted slightly to work more efficiently. Once you understand that, you will discover when it's time to turn the process upside down and introduce a new approach. Only then will you be in a position to drive change through disruption. You need to be confident that the principles you are building upon are important enough to transcend solutions of the past.

With technology dominating every aspect of millennials' lives, it is important that we acknowledge how disruption serves us as leaders. For instance, Jihan took the lead by consulting with startups that bring disruption and innovation to the tech space. Many tech startups need guidance on how to incorporate their business, establish terms and conditions of their services and create privacy policies. Jihan had that expertise and—with regard for the way tech startups disrupt business by improving and enhancing everyday life—took the chance to be part of the disruption by lending her expertise.

It may be assumed that millennials feel less empowered to take on risk and adversity and have difficulty adapting to change but overall we have become more resilient when experiencing failure. More so than other generations, millennials are more comfortable with disruption in business and community because we feel empowered in collaborative spaces that allow us to learn, grow and be productive.

We don't have to originate ideas to disrupt them but we should have a clear vision for evaluating the reasons and methods of disruption.

Disruption happens when we make the best use of ideas no matter whom they belong to. Not every idea will instantly create disruption but small, incremental change will eventually lead to transformation.

Disruption causes us to experiment and learn. When you discover a process needs improvement your willingness to try new things should peak and your desire to learn should shoot through the roof.

Disruption causes us to run a risk. Interrupting a process in attempt to make it better might cause an immediate reaction to failure. Avoid that reaction by remembering that disruption could yield a negative return, so keep your tolerance for risk low and your motivation for improvement high. Realign your expectations, experiment freely and keep testing your ideas.

Disruption could also cause you to collaborate. Sometimes, the process of rebuilding calls for a valued network. You have a great idea to introduce a new project or revitalize an old system but may need insight from someone who has the relationships and knowledge you may be missing. The dynamics of your network could be the very thing needed for your idea to prove successful.

Do you have a fire in your belly? Is there something in business or community that you'd like to see improved through interruption? Disruption is less about wishing for change and more about fighting for change. We all have the ability to look at the structure of a system and determine how it can be better. We all have the opportunity to effectively work toward a vision. When you have the audacity to lead and accelerate change, you've reached the inevitable point of disruption.

THE INTIMIDATION OF INNOVATION

Uber is the world's largest taxi company that owns no automotive vehicles. Facebook is the world's most popular media owner that creates no content. Airbnb is the world's largest accommodation provider that owns no real estate.

We often think of innovation as a mysterious phenomenon that only wild-haired geniuses can comprehend. We believe innovation is the be-all-end-all. We see innovation as a serendipitous force that brings miraculous ideas into plain old regular spaces. The problem with those misconceptions is that, while we recognize the importance of being open to innovation in the world around us, rarely do we see our role in creating it for our own lives.

Innovation involves taking ideas to unexpected places. Innovation can happen through invention or investment. Innovation requires strong leaders who build great relationships and communicate effectively. Innovation requires connections and partners who know how to solve problems and disrupt processes. It's about what's new and what's next. Innovation is also about finding out what works by leaping into uncharted territory.

Everyday people throughout the world are working to meet their own needs and those of others. Whether influenced by scarcity and hardship, we innovate in response to new challenges or new opportunities that emerge. Innovation is changing how we think and giving us new options for how we connect with others, share information and accomplish our work.

For millennials, innovation requires the involvement of leaders who can use technology to convert creativity into productivity. Millennials have a legitimate role to play in the innovation of leadership. The cultural shift of innovation forces millennials to the frontline of leadership. As our generation becomes a force in the workplace, we are depended on to develop new definitions of innovation, making it is just as important as revenue and profits.

As millennials think and lead differently, we can find innovators who choose to make their mark from within. These are the problem solvers and disruptors. They are less likely to be as well known as your favorite celebrity and more likely to more reliable, patient and tactful than the average person. Rather than force their way, millennials learn how to introduce and diffuse ideas through intellect, wisdom and compassion.

Millennial Ashley Nealy is an innovator working in technology. She once visited a middle school in inner city Atlanta to talk to kids about her career path and found that almost none of the students had heard about STEM, an acronym for Science, Technology, Engineering and Mathematics. This surprised Ashley because she had been fascinated with the discipline from the time her family bought its first computer. By the time she entered high school, Ashley's interest turned to passion when she entered a class led by a computer programming teacher who became a mentor.

Her teacher advised her to stick with computer science because of the lack of women in the field and the very few African-Americans who worked in the space. She did, and years later when she visited a high school she couldn't understand the lack of interest among the young kids.

"Everyone could raise their hands when asked if they had a favorite website or mobile app but for some reason, they didn't make the connection to web and app development as an actual job," Ashley says. "A career in STEM is the foundation for much of the innovation those kids have experienced. I wanted to find a way to help them see how they could create innovation themselves."

Ashley first thought about starting a scholarship for girls in STEM, but recognized that it could only reach an individual or a small group of girls. "I thought back to when I was in high school," Ashley says. "With a just a little inspiration from an engaging and encouraging teacher, I decided to take on a career in tech. Imagine if that kind of excitement about innovation was instilled across all schools?"

Ashley began to encourage kids to innovate by establishing the Ashley Nealy A.T.O.M.S. Center Fund at Kennesaw State University, her alma mater. The fund was created to advance the teaching of science and mathematics in K-12 schools through the state of Georgia. The fund provides tools and resources for schools for kids to learn basic skills in STEM and prepare them to choose careers in the related field.

"The lack of gender and ethnic diversity in STEM made attempts at innovation seem intimidating," Ashley said, adding that STEM careers are portrayed in the media as the domain of geeks and white males. You may see Asian or Middle Eastern men, too, but you don't see many women or African-Americans being represented in the workforce as the brains behind innovation. My hope is to shift that by introducing innovation in a way that gets kids excited about their future."

In addition to her philanthropic efforts, Ashley also commits herself to expanding the face of STEM. From hundreds of applicants she was selected to serve on the Inaugural Millennial Advisory Panel for the Atlanta Regional Commission, which seeks millennial input on the region's 25-year strategic plan. She also maintains a leadership position with Women in Technology, a professional organization, where she is responsible for interacting with students to increase their connection to colleges and universities across Atlanta.

Ashley's day job is working for the United States Department of Treasury, leading web and application development services that protect the integrity of the nation's taxpayer system. On nights and weekends, she is running her creative solutions company, Mindly Maven. She's also been named one of "5 Female Web Developers You Should Follow on Twitter."

Through both her job and her side gigs, Ashley has found that real innovation comes from a yearning for change. "I wanted to empower others and create solutions in design and technology to help better my community," she said. "I knew there were people I wanted to help so I funneled my financial resources into those community efforts and stayed prepared by repurposing my skills to influence new ideas."

To tap into ideas for innovation, Ashley encourages millennials to expand their networks. Upon moving to Atlanta, she discovered the Urban League of Greater Atlanta Young Professionals, an organization comprised of young professionals ages 21 to 40 dedicated to fulfilling the mission of the oldest and largest community-based movement in the nation, the National Urban League.

She went to a meeting and was happy to see people engaged with one another's ideas. She soon became VP of the organization and attributes her success as an entrepreneur to her involvement in the Urban League. "One of the untapped sources for innovation is the success we find through our networks," Ashley said. "In supportive networks, everyone is unified and focused on collective outcomes to achieve success. My network has given me a wide range of support for innovation including mentorship, information, advice, connections, relationships, and visibility."

No matter the size, speed or impact, innovation is about making things better. And for millennials, when we make things better, we want them to benefit everyone. Innovation means that things can always change and that change comes natural to millennials because our generation grew up seeing so much of it.

But change can be scary. The inspiration for innovation is unpredictable and can be misinterpreted when ideas seem too big, overwhelming or unrealistic. Never mind that. Millennials seek to facilitate life success because we've realized we can define it by our own terms. We can do the same thing with innovation. We have witnessed the rise of the most entrepreneurial generation in history. We've seen so many great advances in our lifetime and we have to keep the spirit of innovation alive through our leadership.

How can millennials effectively spread innovation through leadership?

Develop a culture for innovation. Your culture is your way of life. Creating a lifestyle that supports innovation means keeping an open mind about the way the world works. We must lead with incremental steps that make old ideas new again and repurpose the familiar into the unexpected. When millennials embrace innovation and build a culture to support it we demonstrate intentionality in our leadership. Our intentionality is kept alive by our curiosity. It means we go beyond asking why but look at our idea and ask 'Why not? When leaders deliberately and routinely ask 'Why not,' they show that innovation is a way of life. And when boundaries appear, we use innovation to push them by facing the fast-paced world head-on with no fear.

We can spread innovation as leaders at work and at home. Whenever you are interested in improving how you conduct some part of your business or handle some facet of your personal life, innovation is in progress. When you try something that you don't know will succeed or match an unknown experiment with the tried and true, innovation is in motion.

There may not be an immediate breakthrough but experiencing the bravery of doing things differently and intentionally is enough motivation to keep trying. If things don't work as planned, recognize the failure, map out the lessons and correct the problems before too much of your time, energy and money is invested. Share the outcome with others so they can learn from your efforts. Track your progress by incorporating measurement and accountability.

We spread innovation through leadership by helping others innovate. Take a small amount of money or a portion of your time to support the efforts of another millennial who is working on new ideas. Ask your peers what they are doing. Cheer on their innovation, brainstorm with them and be open to what they come up with.

What is your formula for innovation?

Do you proudly proclaim yourself as a disruptive problem solver? It may be difficult to find time to think about innovation. It could be easier to simply do things the way they've always been done. But, doesn't that sound boring? Each time you approach new problem take a deliberate break to think about how you might do it differently. With a pipeline of millennial leaders, innovation will rule for generations to come.

LESSON #2: SEEK TO SOLVE A PROBLEM.

Every leader must embrace the spirit of problem solving. In fact, some of the most interesting companies and innovative breakthroughs have come from ordinary folks who didn't even own a business. They simply started with problem and activated a purpose to solve it. The truth is, whether you have a business or not, anyone can be a leader because leaders at their simplest are problem solvers.

As a millennial, you are already part of something special. We were born to disrupt and called on to innovate. You have the power to drive disruption daily. It doesn't matter if you own a coffee shop, work for a tech startup or lead a nonprofit. Your motivation to solve problems and fearlessly disrupt is the key to innovation. When more millennials embrace that we can make a lasting impact and create abundant opportunities.

Part 3

Ambition, Decision Making, Goal-Setting

WAITING FOR PERMISSION

2011. I became a college professor. Many people told me I needed a PhD. They told me I was too young, probably needed more experience. Going back to school wasn't the route I wanted to take. It sounded good, but I knew that wasn't in my near future. I had a master's degree and I knew of plenty of people who taught at colleges and universities without a doctorate. I figured my goal was attainable with a master's. There was one disadvantage though. Most of people who would become college professors without a PhD were professionals who had years of experience in their field and a level of expertise that would qualify them to teach.

There were several people who discouraged me. They couldn't understand why a talented entrepreneur in her 20s would want to switch gears for a career that most people don't transition into until they are in their 50s, at the end of their careers coasting into retirement. I didn't have enough accolades. I had gotten the idea maybe six or seven years earlier. I actually heard a record executive at my radio station internship talk about how she'd be retiring soon and heading to the classroom. Even though she didn't have a doctoral degree, the university was prepared to have her teach courses in music business full-time because of the experience she accumulated. I thought about that conversation. Here it was seven years later and I was second-guessing if I was really ready to take on this new adventure.

Was I being too ambitious? Had I enough experience in the public relations field to teach the next generation of practitioners? Would my breadth of knowledge with just a few years in business be good enough? Academia is an elite institution. I often felt like there was a rite of passage. I had to earn the right to work in academia. I had to wait for permission to be accepted into the academy. Where you went to school, what you studied, what areas you researched, all had cache. I knew this was a necessary stop along my journey.

I knew that adding "professor" to my publicist title would be a good look. I also knew I'd have multiple facets to my career. When I started my first business, I was concerned about sustainability and satisfaction. I didn't want to get bored or go broke. I wanted to make sure the business did well financially and that I had variety in my career. I thought teaching could give me a few things: a steady paycheck in case business didn't do well and a platform to educate, enlighten and mentor students who were eager to be PR pros. Any student who entered the PR industry from my class would have my stamp on him or her. I was determined to make sure students knew their stuff. I had made my decision to start a second career in my 20s, the kind of thing you normally don't do at that age. I didn't need anyone's approval and I didn't see the point in waiting any longer. I was anxious. I was accomplished. I was ambitious. I was 28. I was a millennial.

THE WORTH OF AMBITION

Becky Schroeder does not like to be identified as a millennial. She's one of many millennials who shuns the generational label based on perceived stereotypes. By birth year, she belongs to the generation but she's never been able to relate to the assumptions made about millennials. She's full of drive, creativity and ambition. She's been a high achiever throughout her life. So it was no surprise when she was named VP of marketing at a privately owned software company in the insurance industry. "I did not imagine that I would be a vice president at 34 but I exceeded my own expectations," she says. "Even though I didn't think it would happen so soon, I was not surprised by the progression. I knew I was prepared for leadership and I had the confidence and skills to do exceptionally well."

Ambition is often understood as a highly self-centered sense of desire and accomplishment. When millennials look at what we want for ourselves, ambition becomes the willingness to push and improve ourselves along with those around us. It's having a clear vision of what you want and the drive to go after it. Finding the right company to work with, the ideal person to date or the best neighborhood to live in are all connected to your ambition.

At the same time, millennials need to be aware that ambitions can send you down the wrong path when they stem from superficial desires instead of legitimate and tangible goals. If we get caught up in the picture-perfect, photoshopped lives of celebrities and friends as seen on social media then our ambitions are coming from false hopes.

True ambition has the power to motivate millennials to be the best we can be, yet it varies so much from person to person. It is an internal motivation and drive to continually challenge yourself. Progressing in a job you are interested in and passionate about is a result of ambition. Achieving your goals in life without impairing your integrity or ethics is at the cornerstone of ambition. Understanding how ambition drives the millennial generation is an important challenge for us but one that offers great rewards. Shaping our ambitions comes from a personal journey of fulfilling potential. It reflects our optimism about the opportunities available to us, as we realize the confidence we place in own abilities.

Our personal ambitions may also include balancing a family and career. Many millennials are taking time to start families. When answering the question, where do you see yourself in five years, most of us are choosing to opt-out of parenthood and focus on career.

According to Pew Research Center, delayed family formation among millennials is a rational response in achieving both professional and personal ambitions. Most unmarried millennials (69%) say they would like to marry, but choose to pursue professional goals prior to jumping the broom. A major factor explaining why people are getting married later in life includes the fact that millennials with more education—a group that's been getting bigger—generally tend to marry later. Most millennials grew up in households where both parents worked. So it's not surprising that a number of millennials reported they see parenthood versus career success as an impossible choice to make and would only view children as possible hindrances to their lofty career goals (DiDomizio, 2015).

Suggesting "having it all"—both family and a career—is an unattainable myth, specifically for women, is an an age-old debate. When considering the worth of ambition, millennial women felt as if they couldn't identify with the stereotypical ideal worker: putting in long hours, constantly swiping the smartphone use and sacrificing free time, Pew says. They also felt that their supervisors were unwilling to support them and their career paths. Finally, they felt there were few role models at the top: no women in senior management meant having no business model to aspire to.

This was an issue for Becky, or so it seemed. "I am one of two women at my level or higher in my company," she says. "I once told my CEO that we needed more women leaders and he told me, 'We have you.' That was the day I figured out what my ambition was really worth and where it could take me as a leader."

Indeed, the female millennial has made major strides in bridging the gender gap at work, slowly but surely breaking free of professional confines and pushing the importance of workplace equality to center stage. Millennial women have learned from previous generations of working women how to master the world of the work while juggling school, work and personal projects with ease. Many embrace motherhood with working mom identities and take pride in their ability to excel at work and at home. The desire among millennials with international experience has never been higher with 71% wanting to experience working outside their home country during their career (PwC, 2012).

The worth of professional ambition to millennials is based on a variety of things we value. More ambitious, more mature, more confident, more responsible - our generation is galvanizing every opportunity to achieve.

Historically, many people believed, and some still do, that you needed to spend a certain amount of time in a particular position before you could really do the job well and gain all the possible knowledge from that position. A key component of this perspective is the role that merit plays. The problem with merit is that not all people learn or integrate learning at the same rate. Some people intuitively grasp certain concepts and can work through tasks quickly and accurately in a minimal amount of time. Other people do not learn intuitively. They benefit from the additional time spent cultivating the task while becoming proficient over time.

The same is true with the ambition of millennials. Some will aim high and achieve quickly; others more slowly and carefully. What we do not accept is a mindset that says that people should have to stay in a position for a minimum number of years to qualify for promotion. We don't believe that it should take a precise amount of time before we can get our ambitions in full swing.

As millennials, our ambition encourages us to take opportunities offered for leadership and senior management positions. We place high importance on the need to demonstrate the value of upholding ethical and professional standards. We believe trust should be emphasized when working with and supporting colleagues. Most important, this ambition is underpinned by many qualities that can really make a difference in business.

Our ambition has made us overachievers. Despite what the average person may think, there's nothing wrong with being highly educated, motivated and ambitious. No wonder we get bored easily. We must have a challenge to continuously learn and do better. Our ambition often may get labeled as self-centered, but what we really want is to get better at what we are doing, take care of our families and have an impact on the world.

Is ambition realistic? It depends. Everything you achieve is related to your ambition. Does the one thing you want to do take a lot of time and energy to start? Does the idea that keeps you up at night take blood, sweat and tears to maintain? Does the moment of your dreams require you to get uncomfortable by relocating to a new city, going back to school or living on a tight budget? If the answers to the above questions are yes, then your ambition is worth the work. Putting in the work makes your ambition realistic, attainable and achievable. Nothing about ambition can be actualized without doing real work.

For Becky, ambition is beyond realistic in the minds of millennials, it's a must. "I know what people say about millennials. Yet, here I am working and living my dream," Becky says. "We have to challenge the stereotype of what people say we are. Your work ethic must prove that your ambitions have merit. Only then can you say you've earned the right to be there."

Our ambition does not mean we overlook paying our dues. Becky enjoyed the time before she became a VP at her company. Although she had a plan, she didn't force way up the ladder. She made deliberate and strategic moves that proved her worth as a leader. It made her thankful for each tough lesson and hopeful for her next win. Ambition is a promise that sets us up to cherish present moments and squeeze the life out of them. In difficult seasons that cause us pain, we should push through and use our struggles to make us stronger. In pleasant seasons that bring us joy, we should be grateful and enjoy the good times.

Millennials can't help but be overcome with the type of ambition that make us overly eager and sometimes a little intimidating to handle. Don't let that bother you. Let your ambition maximize your impact. There truly is nothing you can't do.

> **Tweet:** Bring your whole self to work and commit. Don't expect to get all the perks without first giving of yourself. @beckylschroeder #theOGmillennial

THE ART OF DECISION-MAKING

Sometimes a critical circumstance requires a leader to assert influence for the greater good. There is no time for collaboration, since what's best in the moment can't be jeopardized. Even when people around you disagree, the leader is responsible to do what he or she thinks is right. The risk of a failed decision takes precedent over the risk of relational rejection.

The art of decision-making includes the process of choosing from among several alternatives. We make decisions through a variety of methods that vacillate between thinking and feeling. Millennials appreciate inviting close friends and family to weigh in first before making a decision. We are more likely than previous generations to solicit advice. We've seen the mistakes of the past. We make better decisions when a variety people provide input.

That's because decision fatigue is a legitimate condition. A Florida State University psychology professor asserts that we really do get tired and emotionally or intellectually exhausted when we've made too many decisions. We naturally switch over to a reserve of brain power that pushes us through intellectual discomfort in the moments in which we recognize and acknowledge those time periods when we've made a lot of decisions. Millennials are considered multitaskers extraordinaire, even though brain science tells us that multitasking is a myth. More likely, we are apt to switching tasks quickly enough to appear to be doing them simultaneously.

When it comes to heavily mediated multitasking—texting, tweeting, talking— studies show greater vulnerability to interference, leading to decreased performance. This is why experts suggest doing your most intellectually uncomfortable work for a specific period of time first thing in the morning before you become bombarded with emails, calls or requests that require a decision (Tate, 2015).

Octavia Gilmore made the biggest decision of her life when she became the founder and creative director of Creative Juice, an Atlanta-based boutique design agency staffed by a team of millennials. Like a true millennial, she began working at a young age, designing professionally by the time she was 14. Her talents led her to Savannah College of Art and Design, where she graduated with a BFA in Graphic Design.

While in college, she freelanced by doing creative design projects and learned how to manage clients on her own. She was told by older professionals in the industry not to go the freelance route because of the instability of taking gigs here and there and the unavailability of a company benefits package. The pay would not be steady and there's no guarantee the work would be either. Scared and uncertain, she entered corporate America working in creative design departments for Fortune 500 companies such as AT&T and Kaiser Permanente.

She later took a full time position with a startup company. There, she got to see in-depth how a small business works. She quickly learned techniques in management and teamwork. At the end of most workdays, she was left unfulfilled. She had a feeling that this wasn't where she should be. After about year, she thought long and hard about her job. She felt she could perform the work on her own as an entrepreneur. She was faced with the decision to keep working to see where the full-time job would take her or follow her dreams of becoming a business owner.

"I had to ask myself why was I working so hard to help the CEO operate his dream firm. What about mine? So I decided to quit my job and launch my own company," Octavia says.

Octavia decided to open Creative Juice to provide custom design solutions for new companies and corporate marketing departments with a need for graphic, web, package and print design. She hired millennials from a range of ages and opened for business. If she was going to work hard why not work toward her own big dreams and aspirations.

But not everyone thought she was making the best decision. People thought because she was so young she was taking a major risk. Coming out of school, she had bills and student loans to pay, just like most millennials, even though she saved the money that she'd earned freelancing while in college. She didn't have any critical circumstances like children to feed or a mortgage to pay but she did have the fickle future of fate haunting her with the question, "What if?"

"It was actually an easy decision and the best one I've ever made," Octavia says. "Clients who I had freelanced for followed me into the new venture and were excited that I had launched my own business. They were the first to show me support and helped the business grow by trusting their brand to my agency."

The decision to bet on yourself meets the decision to face failure. The audacity of merging both decisions is a driving force for millennials. On average, millennials formed their first business by age 27, compared with 35 for the entrepreneurs of the baby-boomer era. Moreover, we generate 43% higher revenues and on average have already launched 7.7 businesses, compared with 3.5 for our elders (Petrilla, 2016).

Because Octavia was becoming self-sufficient working as a business owner, it was important to be very strategic about the relationships she needed to build. She also had to budget accordingly to avoid being wasteful with any of her resources. In the transition of building, she still needed to be able to support herself. She knew she would face difficulties in the beginning, but had always been a risk taker who made smart moves and, like most millennials, wanted to live a bold and fearless life.

"I haven't been doing this for 20 years and I didn't have a lot of connections to call and help me," she says. "I had to do all the groundwork myself. I had to network and create strategic partnerships. I had to make sure I had money saved to cover my bills and have enough clients coming in. The decisions were overwhelming at times."

As if she didn't have enough to be concerned with, Octavia quickly noticed the weird looks she would get when attending events for networking and business development along with her team of millennials. The concern of being judged by older generations as a young female business owner gave her a bit of anxiety. She would often try name-dropping her largest client or most recognizable brand her company worked with to block the assumption that her team of millennials didn't have the chops to play in the big leagues.

"When I would introduce myself as the owner of the company, people looked at me strange because they didn't believe I was in charge since I looked so young," Octavia adds. "Even when I would verbalized my expertise, they just thought I was cute and moved along."

She continues, "Some people would think we were just doing this creative design stuff for fun and would try to slash our rates just because we are a company full of millennials but no. I have employees, I pay their salaries and they have families, just like anyone else older than us working in the design industry. I made the decision not to compromise on our prices, not to bargain on the quality of work and to charge what we were worth."

As a leader, Octavia is responsible for assessing current business challenges, forecasting future obstacles and creating a culture of trust for clients working with an agency full of millennials. Any questionable decision can stunt her growing brand and repel the companies that are spending thousands of dollars with her. She decided to lead her team to manage client expectations and shutter stereotypes buyers may harbor. "I really don't have solution for the perception that I shouldn't be taken seriously because of my youth," she says, " but I decided to use it as fuel for the motivation to keep going. Sure, sometimes I wish I was 40, but I am millennial and I am proud of that."

The decision to hire millennials meant Octavia had to create a sense of community among her team members. Beyond snagging big name clients, she's most proud of the team she's built. She leads a group of sharp, innovative millennials who have made Creative Juice one of the fastest growing companies in the industry.

To be clear, Octavia does not discriminate among generations. She didn't make an intentional decision to just hire millennials. She has attempted to hire employees who aren't millennials since many of the clients she serves are older. "It could be helpful at times to have employees who are baby boomers or Gen Xers because our older clients like to meet in person," she says. "We decided we would adjust to their needs and speak to clients based on their level of knowledge. As we intentionally work to accommodate them creatively, we begin relating more easily and discover the interests and challenges we both share."

Decision-making is a virtuous skill we use daily, from deciding how to dress or where to eat to which investment to make or who to hire. The knack for decision-making should grow stronger and stronger with time and shape us into authoritative leaders ready for to solve complex solutions. More than getting new business and managing personnel, Octavia also had to determine how to coordinate legal issues with an attorney and financial plans with an accountant. She tells millennials to stand their ground when making firm decisions, but always be open to rethinking the ways things have been done.

"Though we are forward-thinking as millennials, we can be set in our ways about handling business a specific way, especially if we believe we've come up with an epic idea or perfect solution," Octavia says. "As leaders, we have to decide to take new approach when needed and sometimes that may lead to a very nontraditional decision."

Our willingness to try new things, adapt, bootstrap; they makes us nimble and agile. We use that training to our advantage in decision-making. Our ability to pivot and move swiftly positions millennials for the management ranks.

We won't get a trophy for making the right decision. It's a myth that millennials want constant acclaim and think everyone on the team should get a gold star. We all were told the same things: "Hard word pays off." "Follow your dreams." "Never give up." "Everyone is a winner." It's not our fault that we've gotten so much praise and adulation throughout our lives. Is making decisions harder for millennials than for previous generations? Probably not. Tackling the responsibilities of leadership can be a daunting task for millennials, as we face life's challenges at a greater rate and battle with distractions that sometimes cloud the decisions we make.

We all make decisions we take pride in and others we regret. No matter which way we turn, there's no celebration waiting for us when we make decisions. We serve by leading when we decide to assess failure in light of the lessons we've learned. Understanding how to inform our own decisions, no matter the outcome, can turn our course of decision-making toward effective leadership.

Commit to communicating with clarity. It is a disservice for the person in charge not to give clear direction or remain ambiguous when facing a sticky situation. Leaders know the their teams look to them to instruct them with integrity and intentionality. So, even if our decision is ill-timed or meets the disapproval of those we lead, we still move forward. If you're not sure about a decision, say so. If you know what move needs to be made, inform those who follow you. We value honesty and transparency. We serve those we lead by communicating our plans and trusting the results of our decision.

Take risks by trying the untested. Calculated risks are the decisions you consider worth making because the results, if successful, will be amazing. As a leader, you face unchartered territory. There is no fault in uncertainty. And no, it may not feel safe but sometimes you have to jump out there. In these times, remember that trying always trumps failing. Be okay with tasks that stretch you and require you to go the extra mile. The decision to try the unknown can produce the most rewarding experiences. Above all, the greatest risk is the one not taken.

Strike a balance between emotion and logic. Emotion in its purest form pulls out understanding and empathy. It creates movement and action. Logic in its purest pulls out truth and consciousness. It creates reason and rationale. Purely emotional decisions can lead to mistakes when we're led by our feelings. Purely logical decisions can lead to shortcomings when we're led by facts only. As a leader, make sure both minds, logical and emotional, are satisfied somewhere in the mix. You need both.

Watch out for whims. No one likes a leader who can never make up his or her mind. Even worse, the lack of control when a leader does not stick to a decision and switches up at every turn creates a serious state of confusion. Impulsive decisions have unpredictable consequences that follow. Acting on impulse can be smart and strategic when you know you have to do what's right immediately but flying by the seat of your pants can be a leadership disaster. Don't be that person.

Trust your gut. It is difficult to make important decisions without a healthy combination of intelligence and confidence. At different times, one will emerge as more important than the other. When high-risk opportunities come along, the infinite strength that comes from inner confidence can be the guiding force that leads to a rewarding result. That strength is the kind that you know deep down is leading you morally. And when focusing on a difficult challenge, nothing may be more important than clearheaded intelligence to reach the right decision.

Keep your word. You don't want to tarnish your integrity. When things get out of your control, when you know you won't hit that deadline, when the load is becoming too heavy to carry, make a decision to speak up. You may need to ask for help. You may need to ask for time. Or, you may need to ask for forgiveness. Either way, making a decision to keep your word could be the only opportunity you have to prove your trustworthiness as a leader.

THE NECESSITY OF GOAL-SETTING

Getting clear on what you want out of life is the most important thing you can do as a leader. Our ambition guides us. Our decisions secure us.

Millennials in search of mastering personal development must recognize the necessity of goal-setting. But will we know how to maintain and build upon leadership for the future? For millennials, this question may need to be analyzed differently.

We learned early in our careers that a solid education and strong work ethic doesn't necessarily translate into a secure job. We want more time for our spouse and our children because many of us grew up with hands-on parents. The importance of family and personal goals are blended with being successful in a high-paying career or profession.

Now married, Octavia is melding her family and work goals. One of her goals is to groom in the next generation of talent. "I am now starting to hire young creatives as interns who are coming behind the millennials," she says. "I believe in helping them with their long-term goals and being hands-on to teach them what they need to know. I am thinking about how they are going to change the industry just as millennials did. As my business grows, I have keep my eye out for fresh talent to put on my team by hiring the next generation and educating myself on how they work."

One of the worst preconceived notions about millennials is the accusation that we are entitled. The overt self-confidence among a large portion of the millennial generation could be the result of youthful enthusiasm mixed with our upbringing. However, the word is more of a euphemism for overachievement. Rather than accept the label of "entitlement," we should repurpose the concept as self-esteem. As we eliminate this label of "entitlement" as a defining quality, we can achieve the cultural impact and gain the mutual respect in relationships that previous generations had.

"I look at my accomplishments and I shock myself a bit. I've never felt a true sense of entitlement. I just always felt I was closely attuned to the next move to make based on my goals," Octavia says.

First things first: Get focused. Leaders have to eliminate distractions. Make short lists of priorities. As one priority is completed, add another to the list. Chances are, your goals are not just for you, but to make a difference in the world. People are watching you. Know that your goals will set you apart as an example. As you set goals and mark them off, people will want to know you accomplished them. Set the bar high with your goals. People will follow in your footsteps.

Goals are intentional. They are not passive. There are specific areas of life that millennials should create goals for, including:

- Personal Development: As a native of the information age, what would you like to learn or experience that could expand the depth of your knowledge?
- Professional: As your career presents unlimited potential, what are the specific targets you want to achieve year to year?
- Financial: As you plan for the future, what kind of commitments and investments should you make with your money?
- Family and Lifestyle: As you assess your everyday life, what would you like your home environment to consist of?
- Health/Wellness: As you get older, what kind of decisions will ensure the likelihood of your mental, physical and emotional well-being?

Millennials should set smart goals. Following the acronym that has been used by business authors for decades to describe the key elements of effective goals, we apply the concept of 'SMART' goals: Specific, Measurable, Attainable, Relevant, Time bound. Our goals cannot be one-dimensional. They must be based on movement and change.

Write down your goals. This may sound obvious, but sometimes we have things in our heads and hearts and we never put them into words. The old fashioned way of writing them down with pen and paper is vital.

There's power in putting pen to paper. Writing creates a permanency of words. If that's too old school for you, take your phone and type your goals into an app or the memo/notepad.

Schedule your goals. We always hear the question, "Where do you see yourself in five years?" Plug those goals into a five-year plan that covers specific aspects of your life. Reverse engineer and work backward. Create benchmarks for the timeframe you'd like to incrementally move toward your goals. Establish deadlines to ensure you're not delaying completion.

Make your goals measurable. Schedule time to plan them. Mark time on your calendar to think deeply and set your goals in stone. Don't rush. Think through the process. Specifically say how much weight you want to lose, how much money you want to make, how much time will you spend at your job until you move on to the next one. As you create measurement for goals, you will honestly and eagerly assess how they can be met.

Millennials must build a sturdy foundation for goal setting. Key elements include developing goals by using the lessons of leadership learned from the successes and the mistakes of others. It also includes surrounding yourself with people who inspire your goals and keep you accountable for achieving them; that means cherishing new relationships and creating new ones.

Your foundation should include patience. Don't rush the results. Work to maintain enthusiasm on the path toward your goals. The enthusiasm of millennials is infectious. Enjoy your process and keep a positive outlook along the way no matter how long it takes. You should also aim to always help others while attaining your goals. Be generous with your relationships and contacts. You will build a large reservoir of goodwill as you help your colleagues and friends meet their own career goals.

When you dominate your goals, you unlock your freedom. @theOGmillennial

LESSON #3: DON'T WAIT FOR PERMISSION.

No one is going to come along and say, "Here's your permission slip to change the world." With my first business, I learned that the cliché, "It's better to ask for forgiveness than to beg for permission," is true. The harsh realities of the daily grind can wear millennials down before our ideas have a chance to prove they have value. If we are unsatisfied with our jobs or the communities where we live we find a better situation even if we have to create it ourselves.

You already have permission. You have permission to act, experiment, adapt and pivot. You have permission to be conscious, creative and counter-cultural. You have permission to grow, change and evolve. You have permission to own your ideas, thoughts and plans. You have permission to give and receive, to help and be helped. You have permission to show up, speak up and stand up.

Don't wait.

❖ ❖ ❖

Part 4

Influence, Access, Creativity

DO I WANT TO REFLECT OR DIRECT

2009. Social networking had taken over the world. From the moment I started a MySpace profile, I knew my generation would be the poster kids for social media. It changed the way we communicated, worked, played and lived. It was new, exciting and innovation. It could also be overwhelming at times. The easy access, the ambiguity of messages, the jeopardy of privacy – it would make me nervous at times. I was an introvert who appeared to have extrovert tendencies. While friends and followers saw my image on social media as fun and friendly, they had no idea the anxiety and second-guessing I would experience before posting to social media. As much as I loved to communicate with people and share ideas, I often got tired of the demand to be present and accessible on social media.

Since I was an only child, I was always around adults. I was privy to heavy conversation and learned early how to grapple with issues of the day. The exposure to intellectual exchange made me feel empowered and confident in any setting. It made me a great communicator. It also fueled my natural gift of gab and my extreme love for words. As I got older, I noticed how comfortable I was expressing myself in diverse crowds and offering explanations for the most complex topics. Once social media came along, I began to develop a voice that would shape my personal brand. Though social media felt intrusive to the loner in me, it gave me life as a wordsmith. Since it was still a very new, people were still trying to figure out this social media 'thing." Some people were using it as their daily diary documenting the most mundane details of their day until they learned the backlash of over-sharing and exposing private thoughts. Some businesses weren't using it at all other than to maybe advertise until they learned to engage organically with their customers. For my career, social media became a storytelling platform I used to strategically promote clients and position my expertise. For my personal use, it was place for creatively articulating my thoughts and perspectives. My introverted self got comfortable leasing access to the public. I did not want reflect the uncertainty of a novice. I wanted to direct the conversation like an expert. I soon discovered that I had influence. Whether I used social media to enlist support for social causes, attract clients, drive interest in events, and even share inspiration from my own heartfelt thoughts, people were paying attention and responding with behaviors and actions. The more I talked, the more people listened.

Directing my voice to set a personal brand that motivated followers, friends and fans became a priority. I wanted to participate and contribute to the social space in a meaningful way. I began to intuitively understand that my brand identity needed to be an authentic reflection, not a copy of any else. I had a significant vision for how I want to serve the world and I discovered how to do it through social media. I was authentic. I was sharing. I was creative. I was leading. I was 27. I was a millennial.

CALLING UP INFLUENCE

Influence can be defined in a traditional sense as the act, power or capacity of causing an indirect effect. These days the fast pace of technological advances has framed influence as the ability to cause effect, change behavior and drive measurable outcomes.

As with most generations, millennials have developed a tremendous amount of influence. Our influence, however, wears an originality that has created social capital almost beyond compare. The call for our influence starts with communication. We use the internet and social media to form strong unions with like-minded millennials and fortify those connections offline with valuable and meaningful interaction. We want to meet for coffee, link up at networking events, or have a chat via Skype.

Our influence calls us into relationships. We look to discover relationships with those who have a substantial following in social networks, a notable brand or an authority within an industry or a community with a loyal audience. The strength of this connectivity creates relationships that earn millennials influence as a direct result of investing intellectual capital, goodwill and networking. Social capital becomes the key that unlocks influence and new experiences.

Brandon Frame is an influencer. The Connecticut-based millennial, who was raised by a single mother, didn't meet his father for the first time until he was in college. He recognized how many cultural shifts can negatively affect young black boys. He was familiar with issues related to crime, education, unemployment and drugs. He was encouraged by the advice, "Once you make an observation, you have an obligation." He then decided to follow through on what he noticed and started a media platform catering to young black men, telling stories about their accomplishments in business and community.

Brandon created TheBlackManCan, a digital platform with a mission to actively promote a positive black male image. "I wanted to create a space where black men could be nurtured, empowered, and promoted in a positive light," he said. "As a young, black male in America, I was inundated with images of men who look like me solely depicted as gang bangers, drug dealers, jailbirds, deadbeat dads, or dead before they are 25. I wanted to redirect the image by developing a platform that would influence males to build their critical consciousness through self-reflection."

In effort to bridge the gap, Brandon expanded the website's brand into an event series called TheBlackManCan Institute. The goal of the effort is to uplift, educate, motivate, and empower young men of color. With a volunteer network of more than 200 men of color, Brandon within the span of two years led 24 institutes in 11 different states and 19 different cities, impacting 2000-plus young men. More than 3,000 collective hours have been donated to the organization from all across the country, and Brandon's leadership has influenced a movement.

"The emails I get from the boys and their families are overwhelming," he says. "They see a change in their behavior and outlook. Even the men who have volunteered ended up building together, finding things in common and creating connections. The substantive signs of brotherhood across all ages are amazing."

Brandon shifted his influence to cause other influential men to act on their interests and then moved them to advocacy to help young boys who could benefit from their guidance and mentorship.

This shift of influence is an example of social capital—an important element among millennial influencers. Essentially, we borrow the social capital of others in order to appear approachable and desirable to their interests. In social networks, individuals with notable social capital can be wildly popular, with tremendous reach, while others can be focused on the quality of topics that are relevant to them and some can possess a combination of both (Solis, 2012).

Social capital is the catalyst for influence. A person's stature within each network can directly affect behavior or cause an effect. The influence of a leader causes others to take action. He/she is an opinion leader, writes a popular blog and/or has strong social presence, speaks offline to press or to audiences, and/or has a strong network online and offline (Solis, 2012).

If you asked other influencers in Brandon's network, they would say he's a "role model," "scholarly gentleman" or "renaissance man." Those phrases reveal his social capital. Brandon used his social capital for the greater good for young boys who in some facets of society may be overlooked. This is what millennials must do as the leaders of the future.

Influential leaders must consider how they will contribute to the growth of those they lead. People are drawn to a leader who actually leads, meaning they influence behavior, performance, events and outcomes. Influential leaders recognize that they are designed to be part of a mission that is larger than themselves. People need to see you move things along. The influence from your leadership excites them and moves them to do great things.

Influence comes in many forms: creating buy-in, inspiring, messaging, and challenging. However you use your influence, make sure that at the end of each day you can look back on some change you have made that your people can see and experience. They need to perceive that you are making changes and improvements in order to trust you more (Townsend, 2013).

Brandon maintains a social conscious and global perspective by keeping his hands in numerous things in order to have a bigger impact for the young boys he lead. Leaders intentionally develop those people under their influence. They relationally invest into their lives and walk alongside them through important life phases. When there is resistance or difficulty, they lean into the situation and, when necessary, offer a kind reproach.

"We have to ask ourselves, 'Am I choosing to be an influencer? Why or why not?'" Brandon said. "Be intentional about who how you influence people because you are cultivating their leadership skills and affecting their future."

As a leader, you influence your peers. How do you direct that influence? How do you cultivate it? Millennials must set an example of honesty and integrity to increase their level of influence. In order to direct your own influence, ask yourself: "What is my role?" and "How does my role impact the people I lead?"

Leadership isn't easy. It challenges you in all areas of life. Leadership demands that you grow. It requires you to manage the good, the bad and the ugly. It requires you to set an example for those around you, support their needs, pour into their lives and use your influence for their good.

As you are reading this book, you are proving your influence. You are someone who wants to help move and motivate people to make a difference. You are willing to nurture them through leadership and challenge them through motivation. A balance of two is the only way to have meaningful influence.

> **Tweet:** Servant leadership is a set of principles that creates a more just and caring world. @brandonframe #theOGmillennial

GRANTING ALL ACCESS

Being accessible is one of the most critical assets in becoming an influential leader. Access is the means of approaching and communicating. Access is the freedom or ability to make use of a relationship or resource. It involves connectedness. It creates mutual respect and reciprocal value. It builds synergy among people. Access is the beginning of establishing thought leadership, or using your voice once you've been declared an authority in your field of expertise. Technology gives you access to virtually anyone. It leverages how much access people can have to you and the knowledge you offer to them. When you create access as a leader, you must be clear in your voice and make sure you're not misunderstood. In business, you must use your voice to clarify your mission, your plan and your expectations to those you lead. Online, your voice is your content, what you create, like and share.

While influence is at the heart of an idea, access is the way we amplify an idea. Millennials have changed the means and speed by which ideas are validated and exchanged. Our generation's connectedness keeps marketers on their toes and demands that brands ensure positive user experiences. Similarly, our connectedness makes us tune into the lives and careers of those in our network in order to give each other the access necessary for shared success.

Brandon used his network to find more than 200 volunteers from across the country. The word spread about the important work he was doing on behalf of young boys. With so many people to lead and influence, he had to become accessible.

"Everyday, there is a reminder why the work I do is needed and why I can't stop—because there is some young boy who needs to access a male mentor or role model," he said. "He needs to hear the struggles and successes in a man's story. When we see and hear about the negative things that happen to some young boys, especially black boys, it's because they don't have access to positive examples."

Brandon discovered that, regardless of race or status, there was no single community that could benefit more from the kind of experience his organization was creating. Whether they're from the most elite private school or the most underserved public school, all boys need access to role models and mentors.

"This is a reminder that access doesn't know a socioeconomic status," Brandon adds. "I don't get any more fulfillment from helping a boy in an extremely poverty stricken neighborhood with no family support than from mentoring a boy of high-potential whose parents are both doctors;

all of them need access to an influential and accessible leader who can help them learn important life lessons."

As an accessible leader, Brandon won't stop using his influence to make change. Just like how loyal customers are rewarded for their repeat businesses, accessible leaders can reach people to build relationships, recruit into their organizations, involve them in important decisions, or reward them with recognition for their support.

Does this mean you must make yourself available 24/7/365? No. It means that you set boundaries. People will ask to pick your brain. People will mistake your thought leadership for the kind of accessibility that is free, low-value and always available. Every single day leaders must set boundaries if they want to maintain influence. It takes a strong and confident person to be an accessible leader. Sometimes, your accessibility increases public exposure to private concerns, such as when you make unpleasant decisions and take responsibility for failures.

"As a millennial leading a movement, I sometimes wonder if I am too accessible at times," Brandon said. "I struggle to manage my time and identify my priorities. Right now it's just me chasing my dreams but once I add the title of husband and father to my identity, there will be new responsibilities. That's a hard thing to come to terms with. You can always keep raising the bar of the success, but also have to set boundaries so you can take personal time to plant seeds and create a legacy."

Granting access requires millennials stay consistent with their voice and focus on a purpose for leading. How can millennial leaders manage access?

First, get clear on your voice. Ask yourself: Why am I saying this? Why am I sharing this? Am I posting for encouragement? Celebration? Self-promotion? When we take a moment to get honest about our motives before we speak, share or hit send, we have better control on our voice and the influence it carries. Second, get clear on your filter. No, not an Instagram filter, your filter is your judgment. Ask yourself: Is there a better way to share this? Is it a good time to share? Even with the best intentions, we still miss the delivery. Maybe you should take a second look at that photo before posting it, reread that reply before sending or think twice about broadcasting that update to your followers. People don't like to follow a boastful, unrestrained person. It weakens access and turns people away. Accessible leaders are willing share while consistently keeping their voice in check for the sake of how others might perceive them.

Accept your expertise. You'd be surprised at how many millennials are reluctant to own their space and authority in areas in which they are the experts. Put the time in and learn as much as you can. Do extensive research, go to conferences, meet with other smart millennials and share your ideas. Start developing your content. Make sure you're doing authentic work. You don't want to damage your reputation early in the game.

Build a following. Accessible leaders realize they can't get where they want to go by themselves. They invite others into their world. They acknowledge what people say, do and contribute. An accessible leader takes time to respond, listen and express gratitude. Use social media to pull trending topics from your network. Match your expertise with people's questions and/or concerns. Develop a voice that addresses the issues people are interested, add a unique perspective, then watch fans turn to followers.

Use your blog and Twitter, Facebook, Pinterest and LinkedIn accounts to publish weekly content. An accessible leader doesn't waste time keeping his or her social media accounts private. You must let people know that you share content often and openly. Keep your accounts public and updated regularly. Keep your voice professional, and let a little of personality shine through. Show that you're a human who's fun and approachable instead of a robot that's stiff and intimidating.

Assess your relevance. You have to maintain relevance through your voice, otherwise the access you grant will go unused. The best way to stay relevant is to be original. You don't want to look like a carbon copy sharing reports and retweets of other thought leaders. Create a voice and language that belongs to you. Make it easy, authentic and entertaining.

Granting access is a service. Accessible leaders demonstrate their influence by providing new insights and disruptive thinking. Granting access is an ongoing process that requires consistent efforts to lead with meaningful goals in mind. Elevate your influence by granting the kind of access that positions you as a thoughtful leader who has the capacity to make people feel that they have value.

CURATING YOUR CREATIVITY

As a millennial, you're probably evaluating how you can reach your highest potential. But how often do you take the time to curate your creativity?

Painters, poets, musicians, artists, designers; these are people deemed creative. We've defined creativity as an artistic ability revealed by skills and talents, but it's actually a human ability that we all possess naturally.

Creativity is crucial for leaders. It is one of the most important qualities. Creativity makes leaders more effective in communication, decision-making and problem solving. It increases ambition, innovation and influence. Creativity has become more valued in today's global society and that ability to channel self-expression is a key element of job satisfaction and retention.

Curating creativity is a bit of a catch-22. To curate creativity means to preserve it. When we think of leadership we don't naturally think of creativity. We associate leadership with control and order, while creativity is chaotic and unbridled. The process of curating creativity takes focus and discipline, but also needs to be free-flowing and imaginative. The more you reflect on your creative skills the more confident you will be as a leader.

To curate creativity with the youth he advocates for, Brandon started an interactive journal, titled, "Define Yourself, Redefine the World: A Guided Journal for Boys and Men of Color." He wanted to figure out how to promote positive images and make them tangible for young boys. He started keeping a journal he was 25 and found encouragement and balance through the creativity of writing. He figured the most creative method of expression for young boys would be through the curation of words.

"Boys are not always taught to express themselves. We then grow up as men who suppress our thoughts and hold things in and eventually become leaders who struggle to see creativity in our everyday lives or use it the workplace," Brandon said. "When you express yourself creatively, you become a leader that people see as real and authentic."

Creativity allows people to identify with your personality and style as being similar to their own. They are inspired by it. They are encouraged to know they are not alone in their uniqueness. When leaders try to hide their flaws, weaknesses and insecurities, they lose an opportunity to curate connections that breed creativity. That tends to result in two harmful results: those you follow can admire you to the point of jealousy or they perceive you as perfect and they want nothing to do with you. When you use your creativity to expose personal struggles and professional pains you show vulnerability and others began to understand you.

Creativity also helps millennials improve their emotional intelligence, qualities that encompass understanding one's feelings, empathy for others and the regulation of emotions. This type of intelligence has to do with the ability to connect with people and understand their emotions. Emotional intelligence is not learned from most formal curricula in schools or universities. Nor does it get mentioned often as something that needs to be developed in order to be effective in leadership or in life. Most good leaders are alike in one essential way: they have a high degree of emotional intelligence (Miller, 2012).

When we take time curate creative expression, we build self-awareness and self-regulation, two essential components for emotional intelligence. Self-awareness gives you the ability to understand your emotions, strengths, weaknesses, drives, values and goals. Self-regulation involves the ability to control or redirect your disruptive emotions and impulses and adapt to changing circumstances (Miller, 2012).

We assume millennials know all there is to know about creativity. Our generation has curated creativity from the moment we arrived. Our originality keeps our expression free but we must avoid being educated out of creative capacities. The best way to help people curate creativity is to expose it. When we decide to expose our creativity we authenticate a sense of self-awareness in others. We are telling them, "Be who you are." This is a great investment for leaders. Creativity allows for an increased awareness of traits and abilities. Not only does curating creativity foster loyalty, it introduces a culture of openness so that solutions can be explored to help solve problems we want solved.

Millennials are magnets for creativity. Our culture affects creativity. It is a domino effect realized through human interaction. Don't ever stop curating creativity. As you direct change, keep creativity in your leadership toolbox. You will need it as you reap the loyalty and dedication of others.

LESSON #4: DO I WANT TO REFLECT OR DIRECT?

Do leaders give people what they want or do they give something new and different? Do you want to simply reflect people's tastes as you see them or do you want to produce something that might actually change that? Do you want copy or create? It's safe to offer an idea that reflects present cultural norms ensuring expected results. Instead, you could use your influence, access and creativity to introduce new ideas that directs us to question and challenge these norms.

As leaders we must learn how to give more than what is expected from initiating change. Leaders go where no one else has gone. If you really want to lead at the highest level, you must direct instead of reflect. When we direct change we use imagination to facilitate a vision. People are drawn to leaders with vision. They are inspired to work better in a more purposeful and dedicated way.

Change influences culture, which influences how we communicate, which is influenced by what is actually happening in our communities. If you can direct change by shifting one of these elements you can create and lead a new community.

Part 5

Profit, Passion, Purpose

PROFIT TO FUEL PURPOSE

2014. I was frustrated. PR had become a chore. Yes, the beloved industry that I had fought to get into and earn my right to a good reputation was now a vocation I wanted to escape. It was hard to believe. It felt weird, like I was losing a part of myself. I felt empty. I couldn't quite put my finger on it. No accomplishment—landing a magazine cover for a client or snagging a big contract for the firm—seemed to ignite my spirit. The ultimate reward for me had always been seeing the spark in a client's eye when he read an article about his business that I got placed or hearing excitement when I told a client her company has been selected for a huge project based on a partnership I forged. Not anymore. Where did the love go? I would talk to a few close friends for hours to vent or get some feedback. These were fellow entrepreneurs with whom I could share just about anything. They knew the burden of burnout. They understood the fatigue from the daily hustle. They would encourage me to stick with it. I couldn't walk away from PR or the business I'd built. I had invested too much. Deep down, I knew I was done.

There were a few reasons why. I loved PR, but I was bored by the act of serving companies with the superficial need for consumer attention. I loved running a profitable business but was tired of the endless responsibilities that came with keeping a company afloat. I loved leading a team of employees as partner of the firm but was exhausted by how my relationship with a GenX business partner was becoming more difficult day by day. I had no more fuel. I had no more interest. I had no more passion. I had to get serious about what I wanted.

I realized my passion could only take me so far. It was time to start getting serious about my purpose. There were a lot of things I was good at and wanted to try, but I needed to focus on what fulfilled a deeper desire. How I can connect my head and my hand to my heart? What did the world need from me? What would I regret not doing in my life? What could I accomplish if I had absolutely no fear? I had to admit the passion I had 10 years ago was no longer valid. I had to look for a pattern of things that energized me. I had to welcome new people into my space. I had to listen to my life. A few words kept coming to mind: culture, communication, diversity, change and community. They replayed over and over. I recognized the rhythm. These things were the foundation for my purpose. I could embody them in my career and my community, even at home. I decided everything I did from then on would center on those five words. I wanted to remain a leader who was known as a change agent with those five words. Those are things I had to embody, to care about most and to perform the best. It was time to pursue my purpose. I was changing. I was brave. I was resolute. I was 32. I was a millennial.

THE POWER OF PROFIT

The millennial generation is guided by principle. Our respect for principle is more powerful than we've seen with previous generations that have put profit before principle above all else.

According to the 2015 Millennial Consumer Trend Study, 75% of millennials want companies to give back to society. We aim to have an exceptional impact. We use that as motivation to build our businesses for profitability. Millennials have our minds set on the long term, creating sustainable business rather than just looking at generating a profit as the chief measure of business success. In fact, our entrepreneurial motivation carries a strong societal dimension. Today's millennial leaders are committed toward combining profits with sustainable development through social entrepreneurship.

A social entrepreneur is someone who has a social or cultural mission at the core of his or her life. Social entrepreneurs are in pursuit of new models for change. They create organizations where any profit generated is seen as a means to that end. They work to harness the power of business to serve the unmet needs of society. They come in several varieties and work in diverse surroundings.

Social entrepreneur Edward Bogard birthed one of the world's first nonprofit shoe design companies, which distributes shoes to those in need and works toward saving and changing lives. Edward's organization, SoGiv, has adopted 20 charitable causes it believes can make the biggest impact on the quality of lives and communities. Many companies do a similar model but they are not nonprofit. Edward is a philanthropic designer who creates shoes that aren't branded for their company but for their cause of choice, a unique concept that gives globally, generates proceeds and raises awareness.

For every pair of custom shoes sold, SoGiv's gives back to charities and nonprofits around the world. A percentage of profits from every purchase goes toward select charities, many based in his hometown of Memphis. SoGiv's philanthropic causes include feeding the homeless, helping victims of natural disasters, working to stop animal cruelty, mentoring at-risk youth, supporting veterans, sponsoring underprivileged children in need and providing medical care to the community through partnerships with various organizations.

"We select organizations that align to our causes and we design one-of-a-kind shoes that reflect their logo and promote their mission. We donate 100% of the proceeds from every pair of shoes we sell in order to initiate, grow and sustain these organizations," Edward says. "The formula is simple, but the impact is huge."

Edward, like many millennials, is choosing purpose over profit. The power of profit is used by social entrepreneurs who develop innovative business models by blending traditional capitalism with solutions that purposely address the long-term needs of our planet. They are tackling chronic social problems, ranging from clean water delivery in sub-Saharan Africa to agricultural transformation in East Asia and after-school tutoring in the United States. They are working in close collaboration with local communities and groundbreaking innovations by modeling partnerships with government agencies, companies, and traditional charities.

Growing up, Edward's mom would take all the clothes he had out-grown, and even some that were still in season, and give them to other kids. He couldn't quite understand her motives, but his mother was plant-ing a seed for a philosophy of philanthropy. This was an early lesson in playing it forward. "I didn't understand what she was doing at the time but she was teaching me at a very early age how to give to those who may not be as fortunate as I was. It stuck with me through adulthood," Edward says.

Edward's dad taught him how to appreciate and love art. "My artistic in-spiration comes from my dad," Edward says. "He was an amazing artist who could draw all of my favorite comics that looked exactly like the originals. Our relationship helped me discover my purpose by using my God given talent."

Merging art and philanthropy, Edward is making a difference. The shoe he designed for the Mid-South Food Bank has provided more than 10,000 meals; one pair of shoes provided over 150 meals throughout Memphis and the surrounding areas alone. Edward developed a business model to create the tax-deductible shoe at a retail price of $50. For every dollar spent on the shoe, three meals are provided.

"This is a true measure of where the profits are going and to see the real impact in the community," Edward says. "We built a brand that is new, different and out of the box, so we replicate the process and do it over and over for causes we care about. Many major corporations have come to us impressed with the work we've done so I keep trying to change the world one design at a time."

SoGiv partners with companies such as Hilton Worldwide, Kroger's, Starbucks and Westin Hotel, so none of SoGiv's recipients have to contribute out of pocket costs to produce the designs and can keep all the profit from shoes sold.

Corporate partnerships are key relationships for Edward as a millennial operating a social venture. As consumers, the millennial generation values brands that have a sense of philanthropy and social justice. Millennials expect companies to be good for society. We love brands that support their local communities and would rather purchase from them than competitors that don't. Not until recently did people support nonprofits and associations for more reasons than being the right thing to do. That's why millennials question the efficiency and effectiveness of associations and nonprofits. We want answers. We want to know that donations and contributions are going directly to those in need.

In 2013, 87% of millennials donated to charity, according to the Millennial Impact Report by consulting firm Achieve. Our generation has been building business models that deploy technology and enable networking in order to raise funds. We're more likely to use crowdfunding to support charities than previous generations. Fundly, a crowdfunding website which supports non-profits and charities, found that 58% of its users are 34 or younger. Millennials also support individuals during their times of need through crowdfunding because it allows us to do something for others and donate with ease via an online transaction. Crowdfunding is also a way for millennials to use social media to share their cool business ideas and support the charities we care about.

A surge of social ventures like SoGiv have emerged in great numbers with different goals but with similar models—a nonprofit that comfortably supports a small team of employees who have entrepreneurial spirits and philanthropic hearts. These new, smaller ventures have realistic, long-term growth. Sixty-nine percent are profitable and reach profitability in 2.5 years on average. Some are fully funded through donations and grants while others get venture capital investors to sign on (Millennial Impact Report, 2013).

"As the leader of a social venture, you absolutely have to be crystal clear about who you are, what you do, for whom and how your results are measured," Edward says. "Millennials have such a power to create and support social ventures. It's amazing to see the power of profit at work when people give to a venture that you created to help communities and change lives."

The power of profit has exploded through online giving, which enables millennials to have a convenient method to support organizations they appreciate. Online giving offers a chance for millennial donors to inquire about whether they are having a real impact on people's lives. Social ventures also use the power of profit by relying on millennials to engage their peers in efforts to raise funds. Millennials may also direct gifts toward their interests and participate in experiential programs and trips to see the tangible results of their gifts firsthand.

As millennials harness the collective power of profit, we invite an entire generation to participate in global community engagement. No matter the size of the social venture or the resources at its disposal, every millennial leader can adopt strategies to shift with cultural changes to ignite the power of profit. Millennials are actively participating in unique ways to help social ventures enhance awareness and reach out to communities. As we watch more organizations reach their benchmarks, we recognize the impact that is being made through the power of profit. The ultimate goal for millennials is to use the power of profit to provide community leadership, service and transformation and affect the direction and impact of the planet.

THE PROBLEM WITH PASSION

How many times have you been told: "Find out what your passionate about," "Pursue your passions in life," or "Follow your passion"? This becomes misguided advice for millennials who are still searching for their path in life. Don't be shocked by this notion. There is a problem with passion. Millennials are following their passion while seeking a work-life balance only to fail in their expectations. Millennials are worried about finding the passion that can increase their momentum and fulfill their dreams.

We talk about passion as if it's the strongest organism we contain. Passions are our talents, hobbies and inspirations. Passions are temporary deposits of inspiration that we withdraw throughout certain points of our life. Your interests today can become afterthoughts tomorrow. What fascinates you right now will probably bore you to death in the future. Passions are not permanent and generally have an expiration date. They cannot be quantified. They don't pay the bills. However, passions do change lives.

Edward discovered a passion for designing shoes in elementary school. As a kid, he would redesign his classic Nike Air Jordans, manipulate them to become his own by adding his last name and create what he called 'Air Bogards.'

"I knew early in life that I was passionate about art and design," he says. "The other kids would hover over me watching me draw and design shoes. They were amazed. Their reactions showed me I was onto something."

Edward studied footwear design and received a portfolio scholarship to college. Those iconic sneakers and his ability to recreate them inspired his passion for shoe design. When he established SoGiv, he spent a great deal of time studying designer Tinker Hatfield, who created many of Nike's most popular and innovative sneakers. In creating his social venture, Edward made a decision to give back and hoped the shoes he designed for the SoGiv brand would inspire the passion to give to others.

So far, Edward has watched SoGiv generate passion out of the corporate and community partners he works with for his Random Acts of Giving campaign. The campaign was created for SoGiv to randomly choose a cause to donate to and perform an instant act of kindness. Together, SoGiv and its partners have been able to give backpacks and school supplies to kids, sponsor an introduction to HTML class for fifth grade students, host annual coat and toy drives at adopted schools and provide 300 free haircuts for inner-city children (in addition to all those shoes donated).

When Starbucks became a community partner, the SoGiv team during the winter would pass out coffee and tea to the homeless in downtown Memphis. SoGiv also partnered with Lifeblood for World Blood Donor Day to sponsor a blood drive benefitting those in need. Edward has future plans for SoGiv to develop a series of national community gardens and a mission/trip to Africa and to work with celebrities who want sales from their merchandise to support their charity of choice.

Edward's passion for shoes and people is paying off. However, in light of the stereotype, we must address the selfish nature of passion that millennials might hold onto. Focusing on your passions can push millennials into the self-serving, egotistical, me-generation we are perceived to be. Most passions are pleasure-oriented. One study on passion defines it as "an autonomous internalization that leads individuals to choose to engage in the activity that they like." In other words, we mainly pursue passions that are self-indulgent and satisfying. That's true for millennials. Our passions meet our own pleasures but they change. Passion is needed but it's short-term. We don't anticipate our passion changing because often we don't except our lives to evolve as quickly as they do. We cannot make a plan for passion. It's a feeling, and feelings change.

Finding your passion means it's all about you while finding your purpose is about serving others. Helping other people is where real satisfaction resides. When millennials see work solely as a way to accumulate wealth or pay bills, passion begins to lose its appeal in our hearts. That gives us temporary bliss but can eventually make us miserable. We'll soon fall into questioning if we are following our passion in order to live our purpose. "I don't regret following my passion. I hope that other millennials will be inspired by the strategy I took to pursue this path. Passion helps us understand who we are and what we want. But following your passion is a gradual journey to discovering your purpose," Edward says.

Passionate leaders aren't afraid to challenge people to discover their own passions. Passionate leaders specialize in calling people out and daring them to step out of their comfort zones and embrace their purpose. For most folks, being uncomfortable is not fun. It requires soul-searching sacrifice. Making people grow is not easy, but it makes for more passionate and purposeful work. Passionate leaders are intentional about helping those who are under their guidance. There is no way around it. If you're afraid of being challenged or challenging people, you may need to wait a little longer about whether you want to be a leader and reconsider the source of your passion.

In order for millennials to lead effectively, we must recognize that our passions are directly related to our potential. Passion, like our potential, is boundless. You can have many passions and you can spend countless hours trying to pursue them. Unfortunately, passion has the likelihood of never being fully realized, just like potential. Passion can only flourish when it converts into purpose, just as potential is realized with a response of action. When we discern our passion from our purpose, we acknowledge our identity as leaders.

As a leader, you are challenged to see the potential within the people around you and help them realize their passions. Your responsibility as a leader is to guide people to a new level through encouragement and affirmation—where their passions give them strength and perseverance to test and refine their purpose.

Honor yourself and stop fretting over passion. It is a great motivator but it is not a sustaining source. The greatest favor we can do for our entire generation is to let our passions inspire us, instead of relying on them for a lifetime. Take time to align your actions so they reflect your passions. If you find that you're not as passionate about something, then it's time to move on and dig into your purpose.

THE PURSUIT OF PURPOSE

What's your purpose in life? It's a heavy question. You can spend your entire life trying to find an answer. Discovering your purpose is intensely more important than you passion. Purpose trumps passion every time. No doubt about it. To fulfill a purpose requires focus. It requires you to choose the passions that best benefit mankind. The decision is easy when your purpose is powerfully compelling.

According to Deloitte's fourth annual Millennial Survey, 75% of millennials believe that businesses are focused on their own agendas, and not helping to improve society. Six in 10 millennials say that a "sense of purpose" is part of the reason they chose their current employer. It's obvious that we understand purpose. It's important to us. But how do we find it?

There's a popular opinion that millennials are more caring, community oriented, and culturally engaged than previous generations. This means our generation could discover our purpose of truly making pivotal change that stands the test of time. In pursuit of purpose, millennials must harness their passions in order to help achieve a greater purpose.

Passion is the "what." Passion focuses on nouns, but can also be plural. It's about the objects of your desires. Purpose is the "why." Purpose focuses on verbs. It sparks action. Purpose magnifies completion. Unlike passion, purpose is not selfish. It involves serving others. It's about creating joyful experiences for a lifetime. It's about adding value in the lives of others while creating value in your life. It's a win–win.

Edward didn't realize it but he had been working toward his purpose. SoGiv almost didn't exist. He tossed the idea back and forth but didn't have intentions to fully pursue the business. He had uncertainties about if and how it would work. He tried to walk away from the concept or put it on the back burner. But it kept coming back.

"Every single day I am reminded of my purpose," he says. "There is a pressure to address the tremendous needs around the world and determine if I am truly able to make the global impact. As I take time to reflect, I am reinspired to go faster, further and higher. I am reminding myself that this is my purpose." While Edward didn't know much about leading a nonprofit, he knew that if he met his purpose, his philanthropy efforts wouldn't go unnoticed and his gift of design would touch thousands of lives.

In our attempt to affect change quickly, our generation can underestimate the time it takes to overcome cultural challenges. Some of us may throw in the towel too soon. But things get hard right before they get successful. "More and more millennials are giving back in every aspect of their lives," Edward adds. "The response we have gotten with SoGiv, especially among our millennial supporters, has helped us increase our brand awareness but it has taken time for our model of global care and outreach to catch on. We have so much global impact to make."

In our discovery for purpose, millennials send a very strong message to the world that we want to lead with intention. Our pursuit of purpose presents a new way of operating that starts with redefining leadership. Inevitably, leadership will be totally redefined by millennials, as we create a motivating purpose for the workplace. Pursuing purpose is the central force of true leadership for the millennial generation.

Like most millennials in America, Edward, for example, doesn't have to worry about where his next meal will come from, what clothes or shoes he will wear, how he will get to work, or if he'll have safe place to sleep at night. So his purpose became to serve those who do have to worry about those things.

Millennials with meaningful mindsets seek connections, give to others and acquaint themselves to a larger purpose. Purpose is hearty. It has grit. It helps give more weight to meaning than pleasure and solidifies self-control. Most millennials' basic needs have been met—a prerequisite for fulfilling our greatest potential. If we don't make our lives meaningful we will have dishonored and squandered our opportunity.

An empowering provision for the millennial generation is the fact that we are aligned with an era in which passions and purpose are synchronized. As you start with your passions, you move closer to your purpose. Identify what you like. What jazzes you up? What really excites you? Whatever comes to mind, write it down or put it on your vision board. Remove the things that don't matter. Eliminate what's unnecessary. Which passions could you subtract from and still feel authentically true to yourself? Start manifesting your purpose. Take a glance at your shorter list. What do you see? Which words or images are screaming out at you? Your purpose is to figure out how to manifest what is screaming from inside you in a positive way.

We know what we want. The question is: How do we find it? Purpose is a destination. Think about what you want to accomplish with your life. Consider the kind of legacy you want to leave as a leader. Ask yourself what is one thing you would do if you knew you wouldn't fail. 🐦 @theOGmillennial

You were created and designed with a divine purpose in mind. You're alive right now to fulfill that specific purpose. Your purpose in life is why you're breathing right now. Breathe in. Breathe out. You're here for a reason.

LESSON #5: PROFIT TO FUEL PURPOSE

Service is a selfish act of self-improvement. Many millennials have been inspired by a cultural change to create organizations that are neither businesses nor charities, but rather hybrid entities that generate profits in pursuit of social goals. Use your profit—what you gain out of life—to supply your purpose in leadership. Your profit is not just your money. Your profit is your time, your life takeaways, your raw talents and your trusted tangibles.

A large part of leadership is using what you have to grow and nurture people around you in life changing ways. When we lead people to grow into their purpose, we empower them. This element of leadership can be frustrating for the people who are only focused on their passion. We can follow our passion but don't expect it to produce your purpose. Looking a bit deeper reveals a method for millennials to lead authentically, and determine the most expedient path toward our purpose.

Part 6

Faith, Mindfulness, Empowerment

EMPOWERMENT IS ESSENTIAL

2010. I did not like my baby boomer boss. I would say I "hated" her but that's too strong of a word. I did not hate her. Although at times I did feel the kind of anger toward her that could potentially morph into hate. I couldn't do it any longer. I couldn't wake up another day and face her. I had enough. I figured the only way I could get out of this is if Jesus himself knocked on her office door and told her to back off and leave me alone. I felt trapped. An escape seemed impossible. Only a higher power could make life better. Leaning on my spiritual faith, I began to pray to God specifically about my job and the difficult environment. Prayer had always worked for me in the past so I thought it was a guaranteed fix. Not immediately. I kept at it anyway. As my prayers got more detailed, I found myself praying for her; the boss I almost hated had crept into my daily prayers. The peace I wanted for my life was the same peace she could have used in hers. That's what I assumed considering how she treated me and others. Perhaps if she had more internal peace she wouldn't be so cruel to me and my coworkers. Yet the daily stress, tension and trauma in the office became increasingly unbearable. Little did I know, even when they seemed to be getting worse, things were actually getting better. In addition to my daily prayers, I found myself taking in motivation and en-couragement from anywhere and anyone. Because the work environment was filled with negativity, I cherished every drop of positivity that came my way. I watched self-help webinars and TED talks on YouTube. I went to church as often as possible. I asked others to pray for me. I spent more time with the most positive people in my life. I took days to fast from food and log out of social media. I also began to meditate.

Meditation was a chance for me to release the bad energy that was pinned up inside and dig out all the naturally good vibes that were in my spirit. I wrote down my personal and professional goals for the next five years. I read them regularly including Bible scriptures. I spent quiet time meditating on my goals. I would read them in silence and out loud. I incorporated the goals from my mediation time into my daily prayers. As I prayed, I felt as if I was speaking those goals into existence. Suddenly my hopes felt real and my dreams had evidence. There was faith in action. A year later, God opened doors for me that exceeded the goals I had in mind: a new job, new condo, extra free time to travel and take speaking opportunities, improved health and wealth, happier relationships, much more confidence and an increased faith and spiritual strength like never before. I was weary. I was searching. I was centered. I was redeemed. I was 28. I was a millennial.

FOLLOWING BY FAITH

There are lots of millennials who never give a passing thought to follow their faith. For some, faith is defined as an acceptance in or practice of a religious doctrine or spiritual belief. For others, faith is the reflection of past lessons, a recognition of present realities and an expression of future aspirations. For many millennials, it is a tool that takes daily investment to build and understand its power.

For Earlina Green, it was a compass that led to empowerment. Earlina is founder of Millennial Faith, a faith-based movement designed for millennials. One of triplet girls, she lived in a loving yet competitive and challenging environment as her parents raised three millennials at once. While her mother was protecting and serving as a police officer, her dad was picketing and protesting as a community activist. The stark contrast in her parents' occupations created a balanced paradox she would later use as a path to discover her purpose.

After graduating college, she started her career working at the NBA. This experience led her to write and self-publish her first book, "7 Tips to Breaking Into the World of Sports: Landing the Job of Your Dreams for the College Graduate." Soon after she entered the tech industry. With these accomplishments achieved at such a young age, she felt like she had reached the mountaintop. "Working in corporate sports and tech prepared me to climb the ladder," she says. "Everyone wanted to work in sports. Or everyone wanted to be part of the tech boom. But I knew that there was more for me to do."

Earlina started to assess her long-term goals. She discovered she had developed a deep appreciation for freedom and ambition, like most millennials, but felt a strong desire to cultivate her spirituality and share it with others. "Millennials share. We hand down the experiences of what we are living day to day," Earlina says. "We are thinking outside of the box to generate revenue. We are learning how to define who we are by our personal success instead of our professional success. But when it comes to choosing or sharing how practicing faith or religion has impacted us or helped us overcome obstacles, we sometimes get uncomfortable."

She wanted to find ways to open the dialogue and introduce the exchange of ideas about the unedited truths of the millennials and how culture has impacted our choices. "Millennials appreciate the freedom to explore and firmly practice the religion of our choice," Earlina says. "However, sometimes spirituality becomes the elephant in the room We don't always make the connection to faith and culture. I wanted to find a way to explore if the cultural freedom we have as millennials has become a detriment to our personal development."

Led by faith, Earlina committed to writing her second book, "God Of My Youth," a very personal work aimed at helping millennials who struggle with choices they made early in life. In the book, she wanted to tackle controversial topics like pornography, addiction, narcissism, performance-based faith and materialism viewed through the grace-lens of Christ.

"As I write, I focus on the changes our generation is going to face as leaders," Earlina says. "We must have the content that speaks to people and empowers them to seek a greater purpose. We have to have honest conversations about faith and empowerment in our generation."

Our generation's religious views and behaviors are quite different from previous generations. Not only are millennials less likely than older generations to be affiliated with a religion, we are also less likely to openly say we believe in God. While a solid majority still believe in God (86%) only 58% say they are "absolutely certain" that God exists, a lower share than among older adults, according to a 2012 survey by the Pew Research Center's Religion & Public Life Project. However, millennials may develop a stronger belief in God over the course of their lives, just as previous generations have, Pew says.

According to the Barna Group, a faith-based research organization, millennials seem to have a more holistic understanding that theology matters and believe that nurturing their faith is a whole-life commitment. More specifically, millennials are more interested than previous generations in what the Bible teaches about topics such as life, death, marriage, money, or finances. The survey reports that a majority of millennials pray, read the Bible, attend a religious small group, and volunteer at a church on a regular basis. In contrast to so many of their peers, millions of millennials remain deeply committed to their faith and use the institution of the church as a vehicle for social change.

This makes the notion that the millennial generation is lacking in morals somewhat invalid. Millennials place a high value on doing the right thing and maintaining positivity, whether we believe in God or not. The challenge we face is how to harness our energy and our convictions to align with the principles that allow us to make constructive contributions to the communities in which we live. In many ways, pop culture has impacted our view of the world so we are questioning daily how to direct our hearts and minds in response to today's cultural realities.

Earlina believes it's a kind of cultural discernment created by millennials that had not existed before our generation. "The cultural complexities of everyday life are different for our generation," she says. "We are constantly questioning who we are and deciding what we should believe. We are finding that church, faith groups, prayer networks and online communities, etc., can provide us with the mental clarity and emotional support we need so often, especially as we mature and have increasingly tough decisions to make."

She recommends millennials find a church, prayer group, community meetup or network where they can be transparent and express their emotions. "These should be a people who can hold you accountable for your choices and help you believe in yourself," Earlina adds. "They should force you to live in your choices and be accountable to them while also lovingly sowing those seeds of faith into your spirit. It shouldn't be a judgment zone, but a place where you can get answers to the hard questions about life."

Finding your faith is about developing a spiritual discipline in work and life. It's about standing in a commitment not to compromise your influence. It's about overcoming obstacles with a positive outlook against negative circumstances. It's about securing your principles without questioning your beliefs. It's about having the humility to submit to a calling higher than yourself. Finding faith also brings us to pray. Prayer is the place where human beings and God meet in conversation. More than those before us, our generation has faced difficulty balancing the cultural norms of drugs, alcohol, sex, materialism or even social media that could conflict with faith practices. No matter which religion you proclaim or if you identify with none, you can use faith as a leadership muscle. Faith ensures that there is a strong foundation for your journey of leadership. It requires time to build, investment to grow and experience to strengthen.

Tweet: Live in your choices and be accountable to them.
@earlinagreen #theOGmillennial

MINDING YOUR MINDFULNESS

Arianna Huffington. Oprah Winfrey. Russell Simmons. What do they have in common? They seek silence and solitude through meditation. Visionary leaders are known to meditate and will attribute no small part of their success to it. Meditation is simply finding time to explore your inner truth and submit to spiritual transparency. The human brain is an extremely complex organ. Most of its activity occurs outside of conscious awareness. The focus of awareness helps to determine which areas of our attention are strengthened or weakened. When focused on, cycles of worry or irritability become stronger. But if we practice being clear, calm and focused, we would build those areas too.

Believe it or not, there is exponential power in the ability to sit down and shut up. It's soothing to patiently wait for clarity and confirmation. Millennials are constantly connected—powered on, plugged up, logged in—and rarely in a prolonged series of quietness where we are centered within. We are never fully present, neither for ourselves or others.

In the millennials' world, chaos can be a commonality. Long days and nights and busy weekends are the norm. Mindless scrolling, instant messaging and constant updating are the default status. We are frequently plagued by stress, confusion, depression and distraction. We are bombarded by busyness and imbalance. The sustained periods of silence in meditation help us reverse this.

Meditation is a tranquil state of uninterrupted and undisturbed thinking. We often think of it as the final moment of a yoga class when the instructor asks you to clear your mind and empty your thoughts, but it gives us more than that. In meditation, we can discover mindfulness and a deep engagement with the appreciation of life.

Mindfulness is a practice that refines our capacity to pay attention, connect to self and live in the moment. Modern technology has made us creatures of comfort but has given us less time to enjoy the simplicities of life. With more mindfulness, we can see how the way we mentally frame our work improves how we perform. Not only does mindfulness boost performance, it builds the healthy relationships that make the world a better place. It means to calmly concentrate with kindness and compassion and eliminate narcissism and selfishness. It increases the hunger to have meaningful connections with other people. It cultivates an attitude that changes how we see problems in people and situations.

Mindfulness also evokes epiphanies. When we quiet the mind, we gain inspired ideas and can think of more ways to solve and serve. The discipline we need for structured thoughts is the same level of focus we need for free-flowing thoughts. When we discipline ourselves to meditate, we consciously make provisions for light-bulb moments. As we sow seeds of mindfulness, we reap greater emotional intelligence. Constantly checking texts or emails won't create those moments. The depth of our intellect grows into a matured state of mindfulness that gives us powerful discipline and discernment.

You will find that when you are hard at work or in meditation, a burst of inspiration will hit you all of a sudden. It's a one-of-a-kind experience.

The more time you invest in cultivating mindfulness, the deeper your focus will get.

Earlina explores this concept in her writing. "Societal pressures weight heavy on the millennial generation. Exposure to all aspects of culture and overexposure to the consequential ills have a variety of effects on the generation as a whole," she writes. "Millennials often need a word of encouragement or an extra measure of courage in a challenging crisis. When you retreat to quiet place and look inward, you learn how not to be afraid of yourself."

When millennials practice mindfulness, we give ourselves a buffer for anxiety, frustration, panic and exhaustion. You've had to deal with one or all of these emotions under difficult circumstances. Each reaction is a sign of an internal imbalance. Many millennials push through these reactions as normal activity until they crash. Mindfulness allows to us pull away from the noisy demands of the day and seek direction, peace and wisdom instead. We can always anticipate some tensions but as mindfulness becomes a habit, we'll intensify our desire for it and be more intentional to care for the soul.

THE POWER TO EMPOWER

Renowned author Malcolm Gladwell points out in his book, "Outliers: The Story of Success," virtually every person who has achieved success has done so not only because of their talent, intelligence and hard work, but also because of an incredible set of circumstances that has given them advantages others have not enjoyed.

The millennial generation has grown into a time when success is defined by materialism and achievement. This idea presents the assumption that we can take personal credit for professional success but will never have to discover the courage to make leadership decisions that are unpopular and misunderstood. It assumes that we will never have to make decisions in times where our talent, knowledge and experience is inadequate. It assumes we will never find ourselves alone and in need of empowerment, affirmation or encouragement.

Every leader who seeks a legacy of longevity and effectiveness realizes that he or she stands on the shoulders of someone else. Every leader who discovers how to help people find their purpose creates loyal followers.

Empowerment involves treating others as equals. It involves a true respect and sincere concern for others. Authentic care for others empowers them with the liberation to lead and conveys the notion that you believe in them. We naturally respect people who treat us as equals. Treating others as equals lends just as much respect for your ability to empower them as it does your ability to excel personally.

Empowerment involves actively listening to others. Millennials love to know we are being listened to. Most people are grateful to receive the undivided attention of someone. Active listening is the process of hearing, assigning, meaning and verifying our interpretations. It means you have genuine interest in what someone is saying and can contribute a thoughtful response without wanting something from them in return.

Empowerment means sharing with others. Millennials are more than willing to share, but could apply the act to the principles of leadership. When leaders are willing to be open and share their personal stories and vulnerabilities, people feel empowered to share their own stories and uncertainties. We can be desensitized by the number of stories spontaneously shared online and through social media, making the act of sharing worth no more than the attention span we have to spare. Nonetheless, sharing experiences, resources and ideas are worth whatever effort it takes. When you articulate the outcomes of personal successes or professional failures it empowers people to know they, too, can make a contribution to humankind.

Empowerment involves learning from others. We feel respected when others believe they can learn from us or ask for our advice. By giving others the latitude to lead, they expand their own potential impact. With leadership comes responsibility. It's time to lead authentically. You can do so by focusing on empowering others.

Empowering people is not an option for effective leaders. Empowerment must be a comprehensive and continuous process of reviewing effectiveness through motivation, problem solving and decision-making. Every leader sooner or later will face a crisis in which nothing they know or have been through is adequate to inform their next decision. When they make decisions that are unpopular or are misunderstood, they may feel abandoned and seek reassurance and affirmation. We must empower others to act with consistent courage. When we do so, we watch empowerment become the price we pay for the power and privilege to lead.

LESSON #6: EMPOWERMENT IS ESSENTIAL.

Before you can be a real disruptor in business and community, you need to learn to be a disruptive force in our own life. Make sure you're not the smartest person in the room. Greatness doesn't diminish power—it enhances it. Keep people around who keep you on-purpose. Don't be afraid to courageously share your story of faith. Sow seeds that allow your legacy to bloom. Spend time alone in meditation as an investment in your mindfulness. As you go throughout life, focus less on who can help you make more money or advance your career, but more on how you can help others by contributing solutions to the opportunities and obstacles in the world around you. A shift is taking place and it's time we collaborate with empowerment to design the culture we want to see.

The Future Ahead

When I heard that news anchor in 1992 talk about the millennium, I had hope. I was only a young child but I had a vision for the future might look like. I imagined what my generation would do with the world. So much change has taken place since then. Change has been so rapid that our governments, businesses, and institutions need more time to fully catch up. The reality for millennials is the coming of age into an environment that we are the masters of. We can lead, operate and thrive in this fast-changing future. We are better suited than anyone to affect change in the future. We make the rules and create the tools for the generation behind us. We lead with the future in mind.

There is a growing segment of millennials who are refusing to check our identities at the door while many institutions are remaining unchanged in their response to our need for expression and acceptance. This need is not just an expectation we hope to receive for ourselves but one we want to see granted to other cultural groups as the world's demographics evolves. Our appreciation for share of voice is aligned with an appreciation for cognitive diversity.

This means institutions are forced to rethink and redefine their approach. Instead of using the phrase 'diversity and inclusion' to describe race, age and gender in a traditional fashion with no ties to business growth or evolution, the millennial generation has compelled organizations to consider a combination of unique traits to overcome challenges and achieve business goals as the diversity of experience and the inclusion of thought become increasingly more crucial to future innovation.

As millennials move into leadership, a transformation in traditional diversity and inclusion models will challenge past approaches and break barriers that have hindered the progress. Connectedness is part of our generational DNA and breeds the kinds of transformation organizations of the future will command. While there is much work to be done, the millennial generation is a likely catalyst to show how advocacy, learning, and leadership can collectively leverage opportunities to see greater inclusion and innovation.

Why?

Because millennials know that the future is here. It is the world we are currently living in. We can no longer envision the future. The future is coming at us faster each day with the rate of change speeding up and the amount of change shifting at any given moment. The originality of millennials demands that we operate as agents of change. A change agent can trigger growth, inspiration and innovation. A change agent is a leader who reinvents the culture in which they exist, or are brought into, and has a huge bearing on the culture's inevitable success. When a millennial embodies true leadership, change happens much quicker.

Millennials may be the biggest and most influential in the world but we will not be the youngest. There's another generation that looks and acts like we do but they are a completely different segment of the population.

Generation Z, also known as digital natives, are born after 1995. Entering with a fully functional world wide web during a fertility boom and global financial crisis, Gen Z are are children of Generation X. The 9/11 attacks, Great Recession, Swine Flu outbreak, Hurricane Katrina, iPad,

Facebook, and War on Terror are the cultural phenomenons that define them. At 23 million and growing, they will inherit the worst environmental, social and economic problems in history and will be expected to solve them. Following almost three-times as many millennials, this smaller generation is under a lot of pressure to succeed. They thrive on instant gratification, acceleration, independence and self-reliance. They are highly connected to the use of communication and think in terms of statuses and Twitter language. While they are very collaborative and creative, they also lack a community-oriented nature due to social media. They are more self-directed and process information at lightning speed.

How should millennials work to inspire the generations ahead through our leadership?

First, what is important for millennials to note is that being a great leader does not require charisma or likability. Those two things are nice to have but are not entirely essential because they are not sustainable and may not permeate throughout all of your interactions. Not everyone will like you or be magnetically drawn to you. What makes you a great leader and gives you the power to grow other great leaders is how you create and navigate change.

You must have vision. A change agent may not have the authority to make things happen but they have a vision in mind for what kind of change needs to take place and can easily communicate the vision to others. A clear vision will empower people to trust a process not scare them away for fear of no direction. A change agent with vision is able to tap into the strengths of others around them and collectively work toward a common purpose.

You must be persistent. A change agent understands that change does not happen overnight. They are equipped with the patience needed to remain persistent in the face of adversity. To sustain meaningful change, you must understand that there may be a series of stops and starts. In those times, you must not give up on the first try. A change agent recognizes that each step forward, no matter how big or small, gets them closer to the goal.

You must lead by example. A change agent knows if you want to lead people you must have character and credibility. This means you are not just seen as knowledgeable but you are respected as an active learner. You can put yourself in the seat of a follower and ask questions, receive information and respond accordingly. During the course of change, you must also show that you can be transparent, honest and flexible. A change agent is always prepared be immersed in role of a follower in order to lead by example.

You must build relationships. A change agent intrinsically knows the power of people. You must consistently appear approachable and reliable more so than being popular or well liked. A respected leader knows that doing so builds trust, and you cannot build relationships without trust. To create trust, you must be willing to allow people to witness you respectfully having tough conversations and dealing with uncomfortable situations. All of the above, a change agent recognizes that a position of leadership is worthless if you have not built solid relationships with the people that you serve.

Should every millennial have these qualities? If you want to become the kind of leader who is a real agent of change, the answer is yes. Great leaders will have all of these qualities and make a priority of empowering others to be change agents as well. Because millennials desire diversity in our daily work and interactions, we should lead with that same spirit by developing an adaptable culture that fosters inclusion and innovation. Growing up in an era of social responsibility, we seek a higher purpose in our work and look to give back our communities. As leaders, we must keep that motivation to be engaged in improving our society through service. Since we are defined by our proficiency and reliance on technology, we must lead with an evolution that allows collaboration with digital natives as the generation coming behind us.

The future ahead will require that millennials preserve our originality. To preserve something means to maintain it in its original state. The authenticity of the millennial generation is timeless. Our originality makes eccentric or unusual people. We exist to create and we accomplish firsts. We produce new things or new ideas. We are highly capable of innovation. We are naturally given to invention. We are fearlessly independent in our thinking. We thrive on collaboration. The future ahead requires we commit to staying that way.

The future ahead will expect millennials to build a culture of leadership that is based on our generation's one of a kind nature. Following the path of originality requires that we bring others with us along on the leadership journey. No one should be excluded from the task of investing in another. Your leadership as a millennial affects not only you, but those who are following and watching you, and the outcomes of your contribution. It takes deliberate action to maintain originality and effectively lead change in the world around you. Your intentional and fruitful approach to leadership will transform lives. In fact, it just might transform yours in the process.

References

15 Economic Facts About Millennials. The Council of Economic Advisers, Oct. 2014. Web.

A Play for Millennials. Rep. Wide Awake, Oct. 2015. Web.

Brousell, Lauren. "How to Help Millennials Prepare to Be Successful Leaders." *CIO.* N.p., Nov. 2014. Web.

Cosper, Amy. "Disruption Is More Than the Buzzword It's Become." *Entrepreneur.* N.p., May 2015. Web.

Deguara, Dean. "5 Qualities of Accessible Leaders." Web log post. www.deandeguara.com. N.p., 29 June 2015.
Web. 1 July 2016.

DiDomizio, Nicholas. "11 Brutally Honest Reasons Why Millennials Don't Want Kids." *Mic.* N.p., July 2015. Web.

"Growing Pains: What Happens When Millennials Become Leaders Of Older Generations." *The Center for Generational Kinetics.* N.p., Oct. 2015. Web.

The Increasingly Affluent, Educated and Diverse: African-American Consumers - The Untold Story. Rep. The Nielsen Company, 2015. Web. 2015.

Intentional Innovation: How Getting More Systematic about Innovation Could Improve Philanthropy and Increase Social Impact. Rep. W.K. Kellogg Foundation, 17 Sept. 2008. Web. 1 July. 2016.

Metrokin, Todd. *The Millennial Impact: Understanding the Past, Present and Future of America's Most Promising Generation.* Rep. Ogilvy Public Relations, 2015. Web.

Millennials at Work Reshaping the Workplace. Rep. PwC, 2014. Web. <www.pwc.com/people>.

Miller, Peter. 'Self-reflection: the key to effective leadership', *Today's Manager,* 2012.

Petrilla, Molly. "'Millennipreneurs' Are Starting More Businesses, Targeting Higher Profits." Fortune. Fortune, 19 Feb. 2016. Web. <http://fortune.com/2016/02/20/millennial-entrepreneurs-study/>.

Smith, Ronald D. *Strategic Planning for Public Relations.* New York: Routledge, Taylor & Francis Group, 2013. Print.

Solis, Brian, and Alan Webber. *The Rise of Digital Influence.* Rep. Altimeter Group, 2012. Web. 2015.

Strauss, William, and Neil Howe. *Generations: The History of America's Future, 1584 to 2069.* New York: Morrow, 1991. Print.

Tate, Carson. "How to Fight Through Intellectual Discomfort." *99U.* Behance, 2015. Web.

The Millennial Consumer Trend Study. Rep. Elite Daily, 2015. Web.

The Millennial Disruption Index. Rep. Viacom Media Networks, 2013. Web. 2015.

The Millennial Generation Research Review. Rep. U.S. Chamber of Commerce National Chamber Foundation, 2012. Web.

The Millennial Impact Benchmarks. Rep. The CASE Foundation, 2014. Web.

The Social Intrapreneur A Field Guide for Corporate Changemakers. Rep. Sustainability, 2008. Web.

Townsend, John, Dr. "Becoming the Leader Whom Others Want to Follow." Web log post. Http://www.cloudtownsend.com/. N.p., Feb. 2013. Web. Mar. 2016.

Wendover, Robert. *Problem Solving Approaches: It Can Depend on the Generation.* Workforce Diversity Network, 2013. Web.

Winograd, Morley. Preface. *Millennials and Critical Thinking.* By Michael Hais. N.p.: Interchange Group, n.d. 2011. Web.

Acknowledgements

I am grateful to each person who believed in this project and took time to read this book. I am blessed to have devoted family, friends, mentors, colleagues and students who supported me with love, patience, assistance and encouragement. I am thankful to the Memphis Urban League for the invitation to deliver the keynote speech at a conference where this project was launched. I am humbled by the generousity of special investors and early adopters who made the publishing process possible. I am honored to share a voice with the millions of my generation and serve as a champion for diversity and inclusion. Lastly, I am eternally grateful for the lessons, experiences and gifts God has endowed that manifested through this work.

Made in the USA
Columbia, SC
24 June 2018